Fierce
ON THE PAGE

BECOME THE WRITER YOU WERE MEANT TO BE
AND SUCCEED ON YOUR OWN TERMS

Sage Cohen

Fierce

ON THE PAGE

WRITER'S DIGEST
BOOKS

WritersDigest.*com*
Cincinnati, Ohio

For more resources for writers, visit www.writersdigest.com.

20 19 18 17 16   5 4 3 2 1

Distributed in Canada by Fraser Direct
100 Armstrong Avenue
Georgetown, Ontario, Canada L7G 5S4
Tel: (905) 877-4411

Distributed in the U.K. and Europe by F+W Media International
Brunel House, Newton Abbot, Devon, TQ12 4PU, England
Tel: (+44) 1626-323200, Fax: (+44) 1626-323319
E-mail: postmaster@davidandcharles.co.uk

Library of Congress Cataloging-in-Publication Data

ISBN-13: 978-1-59963-993-2

Edited by Rachel Randall
Designed by Alexis Estoye
Production coordinated by Debbie Thomas

DEDICATION

For Theo, my fierce love

ABOUT THE AUTHOR

 **SAGE COHEN** is the author of the nonfiction books *Writing the Life Poetic* and *The Productive Writer*, and the poetry collection *Like the Heart, the World*. Her prizewinning poems, essays, fiction, and how-to articles have been published widely, and Sage has been sought out as a literary instructor, writing coach, presenter, performer, and judge. As the founder of Sage Communications, she has been crafting the strategies and writing the words that accelerate business since 1997. Sage is a graduate of Brown University and the Creative Writing Program at New York University. She lives in Portland, Oregon, with her young son and a menagerie of animals. Learn more at sagecohen.com.

UNLEASHING THE FIERCE WRITER WITHIN

As writers, we can reliably improve our craft by refining ourselves. The attitude and approach we bring to our work ultimately define the quality of the writing we produce. I believe that when making the crossing from good to great, ferocity is our best compass.

The fierce writer ensures that the time and energy she invests in her craft pay dividends of insight and evolution. The fierce writer discovers how to come into alignment with his authority, leverage his instincts, and honor his rhythms to become the truest instrument of his craft.

I believe you're holding this book because you are already a fierce writer. You have everything you need—and you *are* everything you need—to do the writing you want to do.

You may not know yet what fierce writing means to you, or how you can reliably harness your ferocity in service to your writing. I'm here to help you find out. This book offers a range of strategies, attitudes, tools, and practices to aid you in unleashing your own ferocity—in writing and in life.

Together, we will explore ways to reduce friction, gain momentum, and source joy from your writing so you can bring forward the words only you can bring to the page and become the writer you were meant to be. Live the life you want to live. And make your greatest contribution.

Join the conversation about cultivating and sustaining a fierce writing life at fierceonthepage.com.

YOU ARE YOUR BEST EXPERT

THE FIRST JOB OF THE POET IS TO BECOME THE PERSON WHO COULD WRITE THE POEMS. —*Stanley Kunitz*

If you pick up a turtle attempting to cross a busy road and try to redirect him to safety, he will likely return to the same place in the road where you found him and continue his crossing. The turtle has an internal guidance system that is impervious to your ideas of traffic. Despite your best intentions to share your wisdom, the turtle needs to find out for himself how to navigate the road's potential perils.

When it comes to receiving advice, we are all turtles. Even the greatest advice from well-meaning people can't save us. We can only save ourselves.

This notion can be hard to accept. We see that our literary heroes managed to traverse the road intact, and we want them to tell us how we can do it, too. But they can't tell us anything we are not willing to discover for ourselves. Even if Stephen King, Anne Lamott, or Mary Oliver were to sit us down and tell us exactly how they advanced their literary lives, chances are that what worked for them wouldn't serve us equally well. Their writing and their careers have been shaped by their fabulous, unprecedented quirks—and ours will be, too.

Your job is to become the expert of you. When you get writing advice from a book or teacher, or when you see a writer you admire doing something that seems to be working, I propose that you try it only if it sounds appealing, and keep doing it only if it works. Experts are useful, but they're not the authority on *you*.

There is no absolute truth but your own when it comes to your writing life, and I invite you to follow your own golden thread to name it and claim it.

For example, the common wisdom is that the early morning is the best time to write. But the best time for *me* is from 4 P.M. to midnight. A good number of experts insist that you sit at your desk every day and stay there for a certain amount of time, or until you produce a certain number of words. Nope. I'm not going to do that, especially when writing poetry. Instead, I wait until a project fills me with so much love, excitement, and anticipation that I simply can't imagine an alternative to being at my desk, making it happen. I don't *have* to plan a time to show up and write, because I know I can count on myself to do so regularly. Yet, often I *do* follow a schedule, because this serves me well in accomplishing large, long-term goals.

Many writers specialize in a genre, and this is generally considered a very good idea. But it's not who I am, so it's not what I do. Has it hindered my career? Hard to say. But I do know that I haven't limited my writing based on another's interpretation of what a writing life should be. And that has helped me build trust with the source from which my writing is drawn, such that I don't lose momentum by trying to be the writer I think I'm supposed to be.

And despite whatever biases I may have about what I "should" be writing, or the work other people are producing that is more impressive than my own, or any imagined disapproval I might project throughout the spectrum of submission, publication, and readership, I have simply committed to showing up and writing down what wants to come through.

I believe this may be the single most important thing we can do as writers.

I know what works for me because I keep experimenting. I stay with a groove until it starts to feel like a rut, and then I try something else. The longer I live and write and experiment, the more nuanced this exploration becomes.

Out of respect for your inner turtle and mine, I do not wish to offer you advice. Rather, I invite you to experiment, innovate, have fun, and notice what happens as you do. You are the deepest mystery you will ever navigate, and there is no better explorer for the job than you.

Writing can teach us who we are and what we are called to say. You become the person who could write the poems, as Stanley Kunitz advises, through the writing of the poems—and the stories and articles and essays.

Doing what is true for you is the path to becoming your own best expert. Keep this in mind as you move down that path:

- **YOU ARE IN CHARGE.** No one is sitting at the executive table of your writing life, issuing orders about how you should work—except you. *You* have to decide what you believe and value, and what you want. *You* have to learn how to manage your time effectively, set goals, know when your work is good or finished, and hold yourself accountable. This is warrior's work, and it requires ferocity.

- **EVERYONE AND EVERYTHING IS A TEACHER.** We learn from the literature we consume, from the advice of our literary heroes, and from a variety of teachers and guides and role models along the way. Trying and failing is a writer's gold: It's how you come to understand who you are and how you operate. If you adopt a habit or technique that works for someone else but doesn't work for you, move on and try something else!

- **YOU GET TO INVENT YOURSELF, BOTH FIGURATIVELY AND LITERALLY.** Writers invent characters and contexts through which we explore possibilities beyond the reach of our actual lives. Inhabiting another life or place in a piece of writing is a kind of alchemy. You can give yourself any experience you need and write yourself through to the other side.

- **DON'T LET ANYONE ELSE TELL YOU HOW TO TELL YOUR STORY, NO MATTER HOW IMPORTANT THEY ARE.** Editors, teachers, writing group members, and publishers will all have opinions about your work. Your job is to listen to this feedback, learn how to adapt it to fit your needs, and decide what works for you.

Studying others and following their suggestions can be a meaningful way to tap into your internal guidance system. When you become your own best expert in crossing the road, you will reliably arrive at a destination meant only for you.

MINT GOLD

ROUTINES ARE HUMAN NATURE. WHY NOT CREATE SOME THAT WILL MINT GOLD? —*Hafiz*

The person you are and the writing life you create are a composite of the practices you choose and embody. Who you are today has been shaped by the choices you made in the past. The choices you make now define where you're headed—and who you become.

Simply put, you are what you practice.

This is good news if you haven't quite fulfilled the goals you had in mind or established the momentum you'd like. If you want to mint gold with your routines, you can start now.

As I see it, there's nothing that a solid routine can't help resolve. If you want to feel more rested, you can adjust your sleep routine. If you want to feel more energized, you can adapt your eating and exercise regimens. If you want to write or publish more, you can make endless refinements to those practices.

The more your routines align with and express your desires, the more likely you are to become exactly the writer you are called to be.

But how do you go about transforming long-established habits that aren't serving you into ones that are? Often it's not as easy as simply deciding to be different. How do you break your stickiest cycles?

TRAIN YOUR INNER ANIMAL

I once read an interview with a large-animal trainer who said that the best way to inspire an animal to do what you want is to simply ignore any undesired behavior and then give a great deal of positive reinforcement, such as praise, treats, and encouragement, when the animal exhibits the desired behavior.

This is the opposite of how most of us humans treat ourselves—and each other. Let's say you have a stellar writing practice, but you have a single habit that isn't pleasing you; perhaps you're wasting far too much time on social media. If you're like most people, you focus your attention on solving the problem or making the behavioral change you want. Right?

But if you were a large-animal trainer training yourself (and I propose that we all are), you would *ignore* the social media problem. Instead, you would devote your attention and gratitude to all of the things you're doing right in your writing practice. (Maybe you woke at five and wrote for an hour three times this week, or submitted to the contest within the submission deadlines, or wrote an incredible sentence or stanza that made your hair stand on end, or led a workshop that required great courage and commitment.) Keep your focus there.

APPRECIATE WHAT'S WORKING

Wowing yourself on a daily basis has profound power to mobilize you in the direction you desire. And giving your attention to what's going right has a tendency to snowball, meaning you are impatient to get back to that thing you did so well, and keep doing it, until what you want—and what you're doing to get there—occupies more and more of your attention. Along the way, the distractions that have intercepted your desires begin to lose traction. So you don't have to *try* to limit your social media time; you simply hop online less and less as your writing life fills up with more compelling and satisfying activity.

MEASURE YOUR SUCCESS

How can you turn a bad habit (one that's not serving you) into a good habit (one that does) once and for all? By measuring your positive momentum. Let's take another look at that social media habit you're trying to break. By now, all of this attention to what you're doing right has helped you reframe the "problem" in terms of a desired solution: "I want to spend the time designated for my writing deeply engaged in the work that matters to me." Then track and appreciate every choice you make to fulfill this desire. Each time you show up at your writing desk, write it down. Every time you spend fifteen minutes fully engaged in your practice, write it down. For each goal you set and honor, write it down. For each deadline you meet, write it down.

It might seem counterintuitive to ignore the problem entirely. But the approach I'm suggesting is simply to flip the coin and focus instead on the solution. By measuring what you've done well—instead of what you need to improve—you're building a case in your own favor. And as the evidence of your positive momentum mounts, you will begin to convince yourself that you are a master at minting gold.

BE FIERCE

Research suggests that it takes three weeks to cement a new habit. What will you start practicing today that can help permanently change the course of your writing life?

BITE THE MONKEY

I live with a twelve-year-old German Shepherd mix named Hamachi. A large dog with a large mouth, Machi gets mouthy when she's excited. For example, during her younger days, at walk time, she would have a friendly nosh on anything in reach—my ankles, her leash, my butt—while yowling and leaping around.

Years ago, I learned to intercept this behavior by giving Machi a job to do when she is excited. Now we keep a stuffed monkey toy by the door just for her. When it's walk time, I say in my firm voice, "Bite the monkey, Machi," and that's exactly what she does. All of her enthusiasm is channeled into biting and shaking that monkey, and I can get dressed for the outdoors without fear of friendly fire.

On my birthday this year, I asked myself what I know now that I didn't know earlier in my life. The answer came immediately and simply: I know how to get out of my own way. In teaching Machi to bite the monkey, it appears I have learned to do the same. I think this is a critical life—and writing—strategy. Because though we will certainly encounter plenty of obstacles out there in the world, we make things so much harder for ourselves by creating a whole range of obstacles internally as well.

Our behaviors and our attitudes are often our greatest limitations. The good news is that we are in charge of these. And as we learn to make different choices, our range of possibilities can dramatically expand.

Over time, I've developed several "bite the monkey" practices of my own. One is to make detailed schedules for reaching my writing goals, to help me see that I actually *do* have enough time to write despite all my other commitments. I know that I will often improvise outside the lines of those schedules, but they remain the baseline evidence that what I've set out to do can be accomplished.

When I find myself inundated with self-defeating thoughts, I often write them down so I can see clearly what stories have power over me. I draw two columns on a sheet of paper and label them "I once believed" and "Now I believe." In the first column I write the negative thought, for example: "I am not perfect enough to ever publish anything." In the second column, I rejigger the negative thought into a more positive and encouraging one: "I will do my best, and I will let editors or publishers decide if my work is worth publishing."

I also allow myself to bounce around on e-mail and social media for a good ten to fifteen minutes when I first sit at my desk, because it lets me exhaust some of my nervous energy before settling down to do real work.

For me, biting the monkey means finding a way to satisfy the rebellious or fearful or inexperienced or undeveloped part of me with some meaningful activity or construct that helps it settle back down. This lets me protect my time and energy so I can stay engaged in moving forward.

What does it mean to you?

BE FIERCE

How do you bite the monkey? What strategies work to get you beyond your own interference and a bit closer to your goals? Come on over to fierceonthepage.com/bitethemonkey and tell us about your best practices. As a community of fierce writers, we can learn from each other.

PAINT YOUR TARGET WHERE THE ARROW LANDS

In order for an archer to hit her mark, the bow, arrow, and target must be in agreement. In order for a writer to hit her mark, practice, planning, and intention must align.

Imagine your writing practice as the bow from which your finished work springs. The target is your intended result, and the arrow you send out from your practice toward the target is your clear plan for reaching your goal.

Let's say your writing practice consists of an hour of writing every day, your plan is to share a solid draft with your writing group in three weeks, and your intention is to submit to three journals the following month. All of the variables are in alignment. The arrow is poised, your aim is true, and when it is time, you will leverage the tension of the quiver and release. The more practice you have at sending arrows toward the targets of your choosing, the more reliable your aim and your results are likely to become.

Perhaps you'll hit the target on the first try; it happens. But most of us need a fair amount of practice. Over time, you may continue refining your aim at the same target. Or you may have a range of nearer and farther targets, with larger or smaller bull's-eyes. Informed by your expanding insight about your work and your market, the quantity and scope of these goals will likely shift over time.

The way we navigate our path toward marksmanship is equally important to the number of targets we hit.

In an old Irish fable, the king searching for a master marksman discovers an extraordinary fourteen-year-old whose barn is covered with arrows at precisely the center of every target. The king declares the boy a hero and wants to enlist him to lead his armed forces. When he asks the young boy how he became such an expert shot, the boy explains that he simply shoots arrows and then paints a target around the places where each one lands.

Though this is not likely what the king had in mind when seeking a master marksman, I think he discovered a unique kind of unsung hero. He found a boy who recognized not only the value of aiming for a clear target, but also for honoring the places where our arrows land. I believe this is required of any writer who wishes to master her craft.

You had a Pulitzer in mind, but you ended up in the school newsletter. You had envisioned a story about a nurse with a brain tumor whose personality changed, but the characters revealed that the main conflict should focus on how family patterns anchor our identity. The essay you sent out for publication was rejected, but the editor made an encouraging remark about a memorable moment. You intended to spend the entire weekend writing, but your kitchen pipes froze and burst, so you made the most of the two writing hours left on Sunday evening once you were no longer standing in two inches of water.

The arrows land where they land. We learn what we can learn. Then what?

It wouldn't make much sense for a hunter to track a bear with a single arrow in her quiver, right? And it doesn't make much sense for you, either. When you have a writing target in mind, the best way to eventually reach it is to fill your quiver with arrows—with possible ways that you might reach the target. The more ways you can think of to possibly fulfill a goal, the more likely you are to succeed.

For example, I know writers who wish to be published, send out a single, tentative story to a single publication, get rejected, and conclude that they are not publishable. I also know writers who create a list of fifteen publications they'd be excited to appear in, and they don't stop sending a story out until they've exhausted or even expanded the list. Even so, this keeps the range of possible goal fulfillment narrowed to a single story. I propose that you think much more broadly.

When you focus on multiple, possible paths to achieving a goal, you radically expand your chances of success and satisfaction. You can let go of the idea that there's only one possible outcome that could satisfy you. Let's say you want to become known for your expertise in earthquake preparedness. I'll bet you could think of a wide variety of ways to become more visible as a thought leader in your field. For instance, you could create your own blog on the topic, post as a guest on the blogs of other leaders in your field, query *Survivalist* magazine, propose an article or even a column on the website of a business selling equipment or offering information to survivalists, offer lectures or start a group that meets regularly in your community, tweet a steady stream of quick tips, propose an article or column to pet businesses or veterinarians educating people about how to prepare for pet care in a disaster, or offer consulting to businesses in your community or around the globe about creating an emergency plan.

See what I mean? If one of these options doesn't pan out, you can simply try another, and then another. As you delve deeper into your inquiry, you'll likely think of dozens more possibilities.

By diversifying the range of ways you might reach a goal, you take the pressure off, see how viable this goal actually is, increase your odds of success, and sustain your momentum toward that bulls-eye. When you pay attention and appreciate exactly where each arrow lands, you can honor where you are in your journey and clarify which arrow you'll draw next—and where you intend to send it.

BE FIERCE

No matter how specific and singular your goal seems, I challenge you to come up with twenty different ways that you might get there. Remember that we each get to start (or continue) where we are. "Getting published" will mean something very different to you if you have five books out compared to if you just wrote your first article.

IT'S EASIER WITH A BUDDY

My young son is of the age now where his life experience is starting to overlap with my earliest memories. One of my clearest impressions from my own kindergarten days is the phenomenon of being assigned a buddy when doing an activity that would benefit from a little extra accountability—such as crossing the street, approaching a swimming pool, or playing on an unfamiliar playground.

When my writing promotion buddy recently forwarded a set of poetry submission guidelines to me accompanied by an encouraging note, it struck me how much a little extra accountability can matter in the writing life. I seek out submission guidelines on my own all the time, and they often land in my e-mail in-box from various publications. However, it is a completely different experience when a friend who wants to see me succeed—who is, in fact, explicitly invested in seeing me publish and promote my writing as effectively as I can—shares info about such opportunities.

Twice this week, my promotion buddy has forwarded me publishing leads, and each time I nearly leaped out of my chair to send in my poetry immediately. Why? Because her energy and enthusiasm invigorated my own. And also, maybe more important, I knew that she'd know if I didn't follow through on these opportunities, whereas she would never know about the pile of submissions guidelines that were accumulating muddy cat paw prints as they lay untouched on my office floor.

In *The Happiness Project*, Gretchen Rubin describes her need to receive gold stars for her good works. She is rather hard on herself about this and works throughout the book to lessen the hold of this particular need. This is valiant work, and it is certainly liberating to release the need for affirmation, especially in the context of family. However, I'd like to propose an alternative approach that works very well in the writing life: Find someone whose explicit job is to affirm you.

That's where a writing promotion buddy comes in.

Here's how it works for my buddy and me. We don't hold hands as we cross the street, but we do talk every week or two, as our schedules allow, for a half hour. We each talk for fifteen minutes about what we're doing to promote our books. We celebrate successes, ask questions, share tips and professional development information, and affirm one another.

As I'm preparing for our call each week, I feel a little ache about the nonprimary place my authoring life has in the context of my larger life these days, and I feel the weight of all I have not been able to accomplish. But as soon as I'm on the phone with my writing promotion buddy, I'm reinvigorated by my own report of what I *have* accomplished when I hear my forward momentum in my own voice. When my listener proclaims sincerely, as she often does, "That's so *great!*" I have fresh appreciation for myself and my work. In short, I have earned a gold star. But an even more important energy source is my excitement about what my friend is accomplishing. Her commitment fuels my own. Her successes are little beacons that illuminate what's possible in the literary life.

I leave our conversations with at least a few marketing and business-building ideas I'm excited to explore, strategies to attempt, and books to read. That's a lot of value from a brief interaction. Just as a half-hour run in the morning energizes the rest of the day, our call often enlivens my entire week.

This is only one possible way you can go about your own buddy relationship. You can structure it however you want, to invoke whatever is most important to you. Over the years, I've had different kinds of buddy arrangements. At times, I've needed to focus entirely on accountability: making promises to my buddy, following through, and reporting on the completion of my work. In other chapters of my life, I've needed to commiserate or solve client challenges and strategic snafus. I've had literary buddies and business-writing buddies. With one writing buddy, I focused on both publication and fitness goals. I consider my long-term collaboration and invigorating friendship with my writing buddy Pamela to be a primary influence on my marketing writing career. Without the daily camaraderie we cultivated throughout multiple decades, I doubt I would still be working as a consultant after nearly twenty years.

The more supported you feel, the more risks you are likely to take and the more quickly you can rebound from your missteps. With a writing buddy, your accountability to yourself is amplified, and so are your successes.

BE FIERCE

Do you have a reliable energy source in your writing life? Is there some aspect of your goals or commitments that feels a bit wobbly to you? Is there a realm of to-do or to-be that could benefit from a little extra accountability, friendship, or fun? Perhaps you need a writing buddy. You could have an affirmation buddy, a submissions buddy, a public speaking buddy, a celebration buddy, a freewriting buddy, a poem- or page-a-day buddy, a goal-setting buddy. ... You get the idea.

I invite you to choose a writing buddy with a specific, shared goal or purpose, and to commit to a half hour once a week, or even once a month, when the two of you specifically address this single issue together. I think you may be amazed at how the tender seed of desire in you sinks its roots and sends out flowers when it receives attention from someone who is invested in your success.

FALL IN LOVE
WITH THE PROBLEM

THE SERIOUS PROBLEMS IN LIFE, HOWEVER, ARE NEVER FULLY SOLVED. IF EVER THEY SHOULD APPEAR TO BE SO, IT IS A SURE SIGN THAT SOMETHING HAS BEEN LOST. THE MEANING AND PURPOSE OF A PROBLEM SEEM TO LIE NOT IN ITS SOLUTION BUT IN OUR WORKING AT IT INCESSANTLY. THIS ALONE PRESERVES US FROM STULTIFICATION AND PETRIFICATION. —Carl Jung

When I watched a video of free solo rock climber Alex Honnold making his way up Yosemite's El Capitan without the use of cautionary ropes, I felt at one with his death-defying climb. Not because I have ever risked my life on a rock face—or anything close—but because I know what it is like to have a single-minded obsession that a lifetime of practice cannot quench.

In the epic struggle of my writing life, I have inhabited that moment of pure intent where one word comes after the next in a dance of execution that requires an empty mind and absolute receptivity. And I am hooked on the altitudes, the feeling that the odds are against me, and the fierce commitment it takes to find foothold after foothold amidst the inhospitable demands of daily life and elusive craft.

What keeps this writer hooked is the fact that the writing journey is endlessly nuanced. The deeper we get in our practice, as we each ascend our own precipice of growth, the greater our opportunity to solve bigger and bigger problems. Though we may get ourselves into magnificent climbing shape along the way, the terrain of one mountain doesn't necessarily prepare us for the wildlife, weather, and equipment failure we might face on the next. Writing one poem or screenplay or book or newspaper article or essay doesn't necessarily lay the groundwork for the next.

This is why I propose that writers simply fall in love with the struggle. When your writing taps into that place of absolute necessity, stay with it. When your writing is anchored in your deepest questions, needs, pains, and truths, stay with it.

Striving to solve the unsolvable as writers trains us for the unsolvable in life. You never know for sure if you're finished, or if it's any good. You just show up as you are and do your best, and this is what's so beautiful. All of us are vulnerable, clumsy, and wrong a lot of the time. That's what enables us to connect with the rest of the flawed humans out there. Love the struggle, and you'll be able to accept yourself exactly as you are, in this moment, at any moment.

There is another important advantage to leaning in to the unsolved problem: Loving your writing struggle is an exit loop from the ego struggle. No one looks good when wrestling a sentence to the ground. And you simply can't afford to think about that, or whether your writing is good enough, and if the people you want to impress are having the reactions you'd prefer. Because such concerns take your attention away from the climb at hand. This struggle is between you and the mountain. If you focus on anything or anyone else, including your ego, you may miss a foothold and suffer a significant setback.

Seth Godin says, "Both entitlement and unworthiness are the work of the resistance. The twin narratives make us bitter, encourage us to be ungenerous, keep us stuck. Divas are divas because they've tricked themselves into believing both narratives—that they're not getting what they're entitled to, and, perversely, that they're not worth what they're getting."

When you are entirely invested in the work of writing, you can exit the loops of entitlement and unworthiness altogether. This throws the doors open to an entirely new way of being, and writing.

When you fall in love with the problem, you can simply enjoy the climb toward a solution—with the winds and the free fall at your back.

You are more likely to take risks in the name of growth, because getting up that rock face is the only objective. This is why I recently chose to write my first short story in twenty years. I wanted a fresh and epic problem to solve: how to move a narrative along through a story arc. I loved the struggle of moving from the middle to the end. My life, I am happy to report, didn't depend on this type of free soloing, but my writing did. I groped around on the sheer cliff of the unknown for my next fingerhold and toehold. Then I did it again. And again.

BE FIERCE

My cat Diablo helped me invent a yoga position for falling in love with the struggle: Write with a sleeping cat draped over your typing forearms and wrists. Try it for yourself. It's not easy, but it will fill you with acceptance for the burdens of love you gladly carry.

You can also share the pose that helps you embrace the problem at fierceonthepage.com/lovethestruggle.

WRITE TWO PAGES AND CALL ME IN THE MORNING

As a writer, your constant companion is the blank page. Yet no matter how many times you face it and commit to penetrating its force field, you might still feel your hair blowing back and every fiber of your being resisting the task at hand.

When you're stuck, I believe the antidote is to write—but not for the project you're trying unsuccessfully to accomplish. Instead, you need the kind of writing that moves like water downhill. The kind of writing that is trying to accomplish absolutely nothing. Freewriting.

Freewriting is a practice of nonattachment. You write words on a page, for a set period of time, without stopping. The point is to generate without forethought, to move beyond your judging and editing mind, to simply move freely across a page. For the pleasure of it. For the momentum of it. To witness yourself in motion, and to discover the knowing beneath your thinking that pours out of your body when you let it.

I've been freewriting for twenty-five years, and I have come to believe that it is the ultimate fitness regimen for a writer. For me, it is the simplest and most reliable way to leapfrog all of the nonsense I put in my way as I try to enter "the zone" of writing. And I think it can serve the same purpose for you.

There is no obstacle in your writing life that two pages of freewriting can't help you overcome. When you feel afraid, stuck, uncertain, or out of ideas, you can simply put pen to paper. Write about how bored or stuck you are if you need to. Write the same sentence again and again if that's what comes. Just don't stop. When you are moving at such a speed that you can't plan or control what's happening on the page, your mind and your being tend to relax. When your expectation is to simply record what wants to come through, you will be amazed at how much is waiting at the threshold, ready to pour onto the page.

In fact, freewriting is the most reliable lifeboat I know to help you make the crossing through your most treacherous terrain. It is the bridge that materializes in thin air to take you, rung by rung, from "I don't know how to even begin," to "I have a solid momentum and will figure it out along the way."

Natalie Goldberg suggests a kind of verbal freewriting, in which you simply speak out loud whatever comes to mind. Since writing, by nature, is a kind of holding on, I have always found this exercise to be a great stretch of the writing impulse. When you learn to trust the source of your words and to flex its supply of language and insight, it will learn to trust you. Nothing coming through is too precious to let go. The more you release, the more you receive.

I like to freewrite for ten to twenty minutes every time I sit down to work. Sometimes, if I have a limited amount of time, it's the only writing I do. But often it serves as my warm-up to set the pace and awaken my energy for a multi-hour writing session.

Once you are ready to move from freewriting to more intentional work, how do you sustain the momentum? Try these strategies for keeping yourself in the zone and your writing flowing.

HAVE A CLEAR PLAN

Know what you want to accomplish when you sit down to write. Maybe your goal is to keep your butt in your chair for twenty minutes, or to write 1,000 words, or to complete a scene, or to generate a first draft of a poem. It's totally okay to change or discard the plan as you go. But sitting down with a sense of intention can help you choose a direction and gain some traction.

WRITE THE BEST PARTS FIRST

Prevailing productivity advice recommends that you do what's hardest first and get it out of the way. But that doesn't work for me at all. It sets me up for a context of difficulty and struggle, and that's not the vibe I want to start my writing sessions with. When you start with what's easy, fun, and irresistible to write, I believe you set yourself up for a big success first—and there is no energy source like delight to keep the writing coming.

REASSURE YOUR INNER EDITOR, BUT DON'T INDULGE HER

When you're in generative writing mode, your internal editor can bring your progress to a grinding halt if she is allowed on the premises. To keep her assured that she will have a say when the time is right, develop a system for quickly marking issues you need to address later. I like to highlight sections that I know will need revision in yellow. Or sometimes, in a larger manuscript, I type *FIX* at places that require further attention so it's easy to use the search function on my word processor to find those spots when I return to revise. Experiment with what works best for you so you can quickly notate what needs solving without getting bogged down in the details right now.

KEEP THOSE VOICES OUT OF THE ROOM— ALL OF THEM

I'm talking literally and figuratively. From the people in your home whose lives and sounds overlap with yours to the ones living in your head who whisper unhelpful words to the ones reporting by the minute on endless social media platforms. Headphones can transport you to an oasis of peaceful sounds or music, while turning Wi-Fi off and silencing alert sounds and visuals on your phone or computer can provide the silence you need to focus on your own unimpeded thoughts, images, and language.

I find that the trickiest voices to tune out are the ones I carry with me. I have a tradition of thanking my unfriendly inner voices for trying in their awkward way to help me. Once they've been acknowledged, they tend to settle down.

DIVERGE FROM THE PLAN WHEN IT'S TIME TO IMPROVISE

Structure is like the road in an open plain: It gives you a place to fix your eye to understand the path forward. But if you need to get out of the car and do cartwheels through the grass, and then get lost in the desert for a few nights, that can be just as fruitful. We all have different needs for structure and improvisation, and our needs may change from day to day and project to project. I invite you to experiment with both structure and improvisation, and in that way get to know your own sweet spot where you feel free to discover and remain clear about where you're headed.

KNOW WHAT'S COMING NEXT

When your writing session is over, make a note for yourself of what you intend to do first when you sit down the next time. (This circles back to my advice on having a clear plan.) Picking up at a place where you were in the flow can give you a sense of continuity, immediate orientation, and satisfaction. When you sit down next to write, you may be called in some new direction, and that's great, too. But at the very least, you'll have a solid point of departure from which to explore.

GET HAPPY FIRST

....

HAPPINESS ... NOT IN ANOTHER PLACE, BUT THIS PLACE, NOT FOR ANOTHER HOUR, BUT THIS HOUR ... —*Walt Whitman*

The year of my divorce I staggered from day to night to day with no joy, no sense of anticipation, no hope. I saw my not-yet-ex-husband as a villain. Our entire arrangement felt profoundly unfair, with the great majority of our family's practical and financial responsibilities left on my shoulders.

Then, one day while walking the dog, I saw a gaggle of geese lifting off together in their symmetry of belonging. As they left a glittering ripple over the still water, reflecting their unison of flight, I was flooded with joy. This got my attention.

Despite my circumstances and my storyline, which kept me circling my own drain, I had managed to lift my eyes to the sky and see something that moved me. In this moment, I understood that I had a choice. I decided that I did not need to admire my co-parent to be happy. Things between us did not need to be fair for me to be happy. I did not need to be well rested to be happy. In fact, suddenly there were no contingencies that I could think of to happiness. This changed everything.

Whenever I started wandering off center into my feelings of rage and blame, I called myself back. Again. And again. And again. Each time, I told myself a new, more accurate story: *I can be happy right now, no matter what's happening in my life.* Eventually I began to trust with every cell in my body that no one could give or take my happiness. It was my deep well, my wealth, my morning sky, with room enough for all take-offs and landings.

The happier I got, the more my co-parent collaboration came into balance. I began to genuinely like my ex-husband again, and he began to enthusiastically step up in ways I thoroughly appreciated. As it turned out, the dependencies were in reverse. I thought I needed certain circumstances to be happy. But it was happiness that made the ground of our family fertile for those circumstances to take hold.

I am a hardworking person, and I was always under the impression that happiness is something you earn at the end of all of that hard work. Yet, in a lifetime of hard work, happiness has yet to present itself at the end of the rainbow I have been chasing. What I discovered conclusively during my divorce process is that happiness will not be waiting at the end of a Herculean effort if it wasn't along for the ride from the beginning.

This fresh outlook changed my approach to my writing life. For every dimension of my work—as a marketing copywriter, instructor, author, poet, coach, and lecturer—I concluded that if a project didn't delight me right from the start, it wasn't worth doing. First, I turned down a new client that did not feel like a good fit. Then I declined a new project that required skills I had no desire to exercise.

Within a few months, my docket was full of work and colleagues that absolutely delighted me. Because happiness was my new expectation, it became my new manifestation. I was still working with gusto. But I knew I could count on a full tank to get me to my destinations. And when my context didn't delight me, I had a new scale and a new perspective from which to make refinements that brought greater and greater alignment.

What does this mean for you and your writing life?

Your happiness is not dependent on your success. But your success could very well be dependent on your happiness.

Why? Because unhappiness can limit energy, opportunities, and connections. When you are unhappy, the good news of others is less likely to energize you. You are less likely to creatively work through your immobility. You are less likely to enjoy fulfilling experiences with other people. And you are vulnerable to all of the bright, shiny distractions that promise happiness but that could detract from what you truly want to accomplish.

What if, as I propose, there are simply no contingencies to happiness? What if you get to start at "happy" with every piece of writing? What would you write from that happy place? What new possibilities would reveal themselves? How much less effort might you expend toward your goals if they were not burdened with your expectation of happiness upon arrival?

When you get happy first, you set the stage for fulfillment. You get out of your own way. And you prime yourself for the bounty that awaits you.

CHANGE YOUR CONTEXT
TO REGAIN YOUR APPETITE

My dog Henry, whose existence was defined by his lust for food, lost his appetite at the end of his life. Failing kidneys and other health complications made food enticing enough to get him to hobble to the bowl but not tempting enough for him to eat. This led to a great deal of innovation on my part to make him food concoctions that were irresistible, with varying degrees of success.

I noticed one day that despite the fact that Henry's relationship with his food bowl had been severely compromised, he still sat at attention beside the table where my son, Theo, and I ate, dragging himself eagerly around to gobble up any food scraps that fell. This led to an experiment.

I filled Henry's bowl with turkey and rice. And I filled another bowl with the exact same food and sat with it at my place at the table. Henry left the turkey in his bowl untouched. Yet, when I pretended to drop spoonful after spoonful of it from my seat, he went to a great deal of effort to consume every morsel.

This went on for months. At each meal, Theo and I would sit with Henry's food alongside our own and drop it to the dog as we ate. The reversal of the rules was a source of delight for Theo. And Henry thought he was getting away with something quite spectacular that had always been forbidden: being fed from the table.

As we were going through this ritual at breakfast one day, I asked myself: How might I use this principle in my own life to wake up appetites that have long been dormant or to shift patterns that seem immutable? What context would bring me running to my own table? How could I shift the context ever so slightly to render my computer magnetic, so that I would sit down eagerly to write, even when I was too tired, or when I had already written for nine hours, or when my son stayed awake until my own bedtime, or when I had a house to maintain, or when whatever challenge or resistance presented itself on any given day?

I experimented: On the day I intended to write the lecture and prepare the workshop I would soon be presenting, I cooked all morning and gardened all afternoon instead. The lecture and workshop were with me, but I did not approach them directly. An idea sprayed dirt every now and then as I released a giant root from the earth. A bubble of insight rose up from its secondary simmer alongside the chicken casserole. Holding my intention while doing other work seemed to be a gentler way of engaging with my material. I ruminated instead of producing. I allowed instead of forcing. I skipped the food bowl altogether and ate with my hands from the stove.

The flow of idea and story started humming inside of me, until eventually I recognized the song. I scribbled down what I could but didn't worry too much about what I captured and what I missed. I tuned into something that I know how to return to. I left the food bowl to enter the feast.

BE FIERCE

What if you found a new way to approach an old struggle or stuck place? How could you come at it sideways to find a new perspective? What if you were to make a small shift in attitude or practice—and then another—until you felt a bit more space or ease or fun? What if you didn't stop experimenting until you found yourself clear to the other side of that obstacle? I'd love to hear how you changed your context to create a new result at fierceonthepage.com/changeyourcontext.

HOW MUCH THE WRITING LIFE CAN HOLD

NO ONE HAS EVER MEASURED, NOT EVEN POETS, HOW MUCH THE HEART CAN HOLD. —*Zelda Fitzgerald*

I am a member of an online community dedicated to mothers who experienced a particular type of birth trauma. One day a poet I know posted on the forum. I didn't know she was a mother, wasn't aware she had a child my son's age, and hadn't expected that she shared this singular type of grief with me.

This woman's brief post felt like a benediction. She revealed her sorrow with a ferocity and an honesty that spliced my shame about my grief wide open. I was sanctified by a fresh tide of tears. This is the power of the written word. As we take in a story that affects us, we meet ourselves more deeply. Our thinking and our choices can be altered by the words and stories we allow to penetrate. And these stories don't just await us on the page; they are the currency of human experience and the context of our lives.

Everything that happens in your life is a part of your writing life. Every moment of every day makes up your raw material. Every life choice you make is meaningful to your writing, and every writing choice you make is meaningful to your life. Following are some ways to mine the natural resources of your experience while stretching your sense of possibility for how much the writing life can hold.

LET EVERYTHING HAPPEN TO YOU

Rainer Maria Rilke advises writers to "… go to the limits of your longing. … Let everything happen to you: beauty and terror. Just keep going. No feeling is final."[1] For writers, writing is the way we keep going. Writing is our receptor and translator of beauty and terror, and every other feeling and experience that moves through us.

The heart's capacity is infinite—and so is your writing life. No matter what your goals, desires, experience, personality, skill, or life circumstance, you have everything you need to cultivate a writing life—*your* writing life—to grow in mastery and magnificence wherever your inspiration and practice lead you.

The truth is, you can't possibly do it wrong.

MAKE SPACE FOR WRITING BY NOT WRITING

Sometimes not writing is the most powerful choice a writer can make. When you can let go and engage in other activities, ideas for new work and solutions for writing you've been working on often bubble to the surface and present themselves. Plus, taking care of the rest of what life demands can clear your mental cache so that your eventual writing time is more spacious and uncluttered. This is great news if you aren't at your writing desk (or notebook or computer) as often as you wish you were. If you choose to stay awake to what you are writing and what you intend to write, you will keep the channel open, through which the gifts of your writing life can accumulate in the background and present themselves when you are ready to receive them.

STOKE THE FLAMES

Leonard Cohen says, "Poetry is just the evidence of life. If your life is burning well, poetry is just the ash." How do you learn to generate such valuable material that you use yourself up, right down to the filter? I propose that a life burns well when you pay attention—and then record it

---

1. Translated by Anita Barrows and Joanna Macy.

just as you see it (or imagine it). There are no shortcuts. Writing and life are long-term projects. The destinations can be ambiguous and hard to reach. But the journey is always full of remarkable images and characters and language.

The writing you produce is the evidence that you showed up at the page, as you showed up for your life. Your practice of presence stokes the flames.

WHAT YOU SAY IS WHO YOU ARE

The words you choose are of the utmost importance, because what you say is who you are. I was reminded of this on an early-morning dog walk as I approached a young couple physically struggling in front of a neighbor's large vegetable patch.

"Don't do that! You are stealing." The woman gasped, lunging between the man and the cherry tomatoes.

"I'm not stealing," he said, twisting around her and helping himself to a few tomatoes. "We're a part of this community, and these are for us all to share."

In two short sentences, I gathered two different interpretations of a neighbor's tomato plants and the act of eating from them. I had enough information from this snippet of dialogue to imagine what these people's life stories might be—and their dynamic with each other.

WE LIVE IN OUR STORIES, NOT OUR LIVES

We don't live in our lives but in the stories we tell *about* our lives. The stories we choose to invest in are the ones that define our lives. Most of us are living by stories that have us by the throat, and we don't even know it. We can tell ourselves we are part of a community and the tomatoes are for sharing, or that we are stealing. We can tell ourselves that the marriage was a success or a failure. We can tell ourselves pretty much anything and make a believable case for it; we are writers, after all.

Some stories run so deep that it can take a whole lot of writing to yank the taproot or retrain the vines. But it's possible. Consider if you are telling yourself an unkind or unwelcoming story that limits you in some way. How might you retell it?

A WRITING PRACTICE IS A LIFE PRACTICE

What you learn on the page can be translated to everything that matters in your life. My writing practice taught me how to honor my losses by sourcing the wisdom gained. It taught me how to tackle my intense resistance to learning to cook. It taught me how to move from frumpy to fit with discipline and good humor.

Writing can even be a healing practice, if that's what you want or need. I have long considered it to be the art of repair through language. In my own literary cosmology, it seems to me that we restore ourselves and our world by arranging the fragments of experience, memory, invention, and emotion into a mosaic of meaning through which we transcend the parts and move into unexpected wholeness.

BE FIERCE

Your life and your writing are in your hands. No one has ever measured how much the writing life can hold. You get to decide. There's no better person for the job.

KNOW YOURSELF,
WELCOME YOURSELF

When I was hired by a large company to write a campaign for a brand that hadn't been articulated yet, I enlisted the help of my friend Sarah. Sarah is a brand strategist, the founder of a wildly successful company, and one of the smartest people I know.

The plan was this: Sarah would articulate the brand strategy, and then I would write the communications that expressed it. In the past we'd collaborated in this way for a range of corporate clients, to great success.

As I sat in the executive conference room at the tippy top of a San Francisco office building, listening to Sarah deliver her impeccable argument about the inevitability of this brand, I thought of Michelangelo. I felt certain that, like a sculptor, Sarah could see through any block of marble to the brand waiting to be liberated at its center.

Over dinner that night, I told Sarah how much I admired her expertise. I confessed that, watching her, I felt a kind of shame. I realized that I'd always believed I was supposed to have the type of intelligence she has—that I was supposed to be the person who defines the strategy, stands up in front of an executive team, and convinces them of something important. But what I love is to write the campaign—at home, in my yoga pants, with an audience of napping cats—that expresses the brand. Along the way, some part of me had decided that this was an inferior skill set.

Sarah was having a hard time understanding where I was coming from. "But you're a *poet*," she protested. "You have deep insights into human truths and can share them in a way that reaches and moves people. I've always wanted to do that. What's so great about creating a brand strategy?"

Her response shocked me. The fact that I might have a type of intelligence that Sarah appreciated had not occurred to me.

It's so easy to compare ourselves to people we admire and decide that we come up short. Whether those people would happily trade places with us is irrelevant; the fact is that yearning to be different is not going to change anything but your mood—for the worse. If you are an apple tree, you're not going to produce pears, though you may have a lot to learn from the pear tree.

I think part of the reason we can get caught up in other-worship is that we haven't yet learned to recognize and embody our own competencies and gifts. Many of us come out of childhood with an idealized version of intelligence or aptitude, one that reflects, perhaps, a particular revered classmate or the bias of a teacher or parent or awards committee. And we live by a subconscious story, which we may never have articulated, about the ways we don't measure up to this unquestioned standard.

I propose that we question our standard for ourselves and begin to dismantle the stories that don't serve us. Instead of judging where you fall short, what if you were to appreciate your skill set, your unique perspective, and your contributions to the conversations you're having and communities you're living and working in? When you have an accurate story about who you are, how you contribute, and what you need in order to accelerate, you can give yourself more of what you need, appreciate your strengths, and accept the ways you're simply not wired to behave.

GET TO KNOW YOU

When I was growing up, a song played during the *Sesame Street* commercial breaks with a chorus that went, "The most important person in the whole wide world is you, and you hardly even know you." This made an impression on me at age three, and I still marvel today at how largely unexplored the territory of the self can be.

There are endless lenses that can help us make sense of who we are and how to leverage what's best in us. I have studied the Myers-Briggs

Type Indicator, five-element acupuncture, the Enneagram of Personality, tarot, character archetypes, and various workplace personality mapping tests to get the inside scoop on myself. I've read books on attachment style, happiness aptitude, mind-set, and strategies for self-cultivation.

The better I understand myself, the more equipped I feel to choose the contexts, communities, and work that brings forth the best in me.

What about you? Are you earth or fire? An extrovert or an introvert? A damsel in distress or the knight who will save her? A pantser or a planner? What's immutable about you? What's flexible? How might you stretch in unexpected ways that serve your writing surprisingly well? And what ways are you simply not likely to bend? What makes you feel connected, and what shuts you down? Who invigorates you, and in what type of environment?

I am an extrovert who works from home, alone. My boyfriend, Mark, is an introvert who is deeply engaged with people all day in his civic leadership role. At the end of the day, when we come together, I want to go out to reboot, and he prefers to stay in to do the same. Because we understand this about ourselves, we can get creative about how to meet our respective needs.

CLAIM YOUR WRITING TERRAIN

As my son has recently introduced Taylor Swift into our household, I have been marveling at this megastar's endless iterations of the glorified, failed relationship. She has built an empire on her broken heart. And I'm guessing that young Taylor never told herself that her subject matter is unworthy. What if we were all so generous with ourselves? Many of us spend a lifetime circling inner terrain that we never fully explore with writing. I wish I hadn't wasted a few decades judging and resisting my own.

I think a primary opportunity of knowing ourselves better is to become equipped to strive toward greater coherence. When we are doing work that enlivens us, that we are called to do, that brings forth what is best in us, and that gives us the opportunity to cultivate the skills and strengths we value, we can make our greatest contribution.

CHALLENGE YOUR SENSE OF SELF

Once we've grounded ourselves in deep appreciation for what we have to offer the world as people and writers, it can be great fun and of great value to play against type. After my divorce, for example, I vowed not to default to "making things happen" in my dating life as I had in my marriage. I wanted to know what it felt like to have someone else make the plans, pick up the tab, and take the lead in sustaining the relationship's momentum. Playing against type in this way, I began to observe how I overcompensated with control whenever I felt afraid or uncertain.

Turns out, I was also trying to "make things happen" in my writing life to the detriment of "allowing things to happen." To explore my alternatives, I watched people I admired, and I tried on different archetypes and approaches. Some didn't fit at all. And some were well worth the uncomfortable mile in another person's shoes, because I learned new attitudes, strategies, and even postures. I'd venture to say that my presentations in the boardroom have improved by imitating the jaunty grace and effortless authority of my friend and colleague Sarah.

How can you experiment with the reverse of what is familiar and see how this might open up new territory in your writing process and results?

Sarah has brand strategy covered. Taylor has the broken heart covered. I'll never be a brand strategist or a rock star. But I can have a good time embodying those whom I admire. Venturing into the territory others occupy could be a useful exercise in helping you discover an unexpected archetype lodged deep within you somewhere, seeking a voice. And venturing into the territory of yourself can give you sure footing and a solid foundation from which to set sail.

Who are you as a writer, and what terrain do you intend to make your own?

SERVE YOUR AUDIENCE

At a writing conference where I was teaching a workshop, we were discussing different types of content that can be shared on a blog. A student raised her hand. "Last night I attended a sex-positive party," she said, "and I'm wondering if I should blog about it."

"That depends on what the topic of your blog is and who your audience is," I answered. "If you are a sex therapist or columnist, I'd expect that your readers would be very interested in your reactions to that experience. But if your blog offers craft projects for preschoolers, I'd hold off on mentioning the sex-positive party—because at best it would confuse readers, and at worst, it could offend them."

Another student chimed in: "So are you saying that we should censor ourselves?"

"What I'm saying is that when you offer a blog focused on a particular topic or theme, your readers come to you for that. When you wander too far from the theme you have promised, you weaken your connection with readers—or could lose them altogether."

I explained that on my Radical Divorce blog, for example, I focus on helping divorcing parents heal well so everyone in the family can thrive. If I were feeling grumpy about my co-parent, this would not be the place I'd go to complain about him. However, if I saw an opportunity to share with readers how I was able to move through grumpiness to greater acceptance, peace, and collaboration, then I'd share that on my blog.

It all boils down to this: When you're clear about your topic, genre, or realm of expertise, it is much easier to attract the people who are seeking what you are offering. When you stay on topic and regularly deliver content that provides real value, it is much easier to sustain connections with readers over time.

IS YOUR SOCIAL MEDIA FOCUSED ON SUSTAINING RELATIONSHIPS WITH READERS?

What's tricky about today's extravaganza of social media is that writers have nearly endless channels through which to share our words. And I believe that everything we say, no matter where, contributes to our body of work. Meaning every tweet, every Facebook and Instagram post, every YouTube video, every piece of content shared, and every image pinned is a reflection on who you are and what you offer as a writer. Even the way you drive, what you are overheard saying in a coffee shop, the way you behave in the grocery store line, and your body language as you walk your dog are part of your public persona.

Participating online and in the "real" world with clarity and intention can help you become more coherent in your life and your writing. Is it meaningful for your readers to know that you're struggling with infertility, for example? If you write about women's health, midwifery, or a related topic, this could be spot-on. If not, I propose that you take a step back and decide with whom you'd like to share this important information. Same with your opinions about politics, the literary landscape, what you ate this morning, and what you think of your kid's teacher. I'm not saying that any of these insights is necessarily off-limits. But I am suggesting that you think about what you're sharing, why, and how it contributes to your body of work.

YOU'RE ON-TARGET, BUT IS THAT ENOUGH?

My physician client wants to educate his patients about the value of IV vitamin treatments. He sends me his two-page flier to edit. It reads like a scientific paper that was written to educate scholars about the difference between acute inflammation and chronic inflammation, and the cells' role in promoting health.

The flyer assures me that this doctor knows his stuff. But it doesn't address the issues I'd expect a patient would want to know.

I put myself in the patient's shoes and asked: What would inspire me to spend time and money on this kind of treatment? How is it more effective than the vitamin pills I take every morning? How will it save me money? How does it dramatically boost my immunity? And why is it worth sticking a needle in my arm to do so?

I invited the physician to offer the same great information he'd already shared, but with a focus on answering these questions. We came up with a new headline as an organizing principle: "Are you wasting money because you aren't absorbing your vitamins?" (That would get my attention as a patient.) He began to reorganize and rewrite from there.

It was a revelation to the doctor that the way he spoke to and wrote for his patients could have an enormous impact on meeting their needs.

The same is true for you. What you have to share as a writer is extremely important. And the way you share it in service to your readers is equally so.

BE FIERCE

I challenge you to relentlessly ask yourself the following questions in reference to everything you write: How does this offering help me reach and satisfy my readers? Is it delivering on what I've promised in a way that readers will be able to understand and use? Even if you're not sure who your readers are, even if you are writing fiction or poetry, considering your readers can help you attune yourself over time to what you are offering. Doing so can also influence who is drawn to it, how it adds value to their lives, and the direction you take in your writing.

WHAT IF YOU STOPPED TRYING SO HARD?

When I was growing up, it seemed as if my father and brother had the answers to every academic test and Trivial Pursuit game directly ported into their brains. I, on the other hand, would spend hours every night laboring over my homework, dedicating my entire being to the comprehension of topics such as algebra and biology, which were nonnative to my poetic dream state.

It paid off. I excelled in school, even in subjects in which I had no foundational ease or basic understanding. I came to appreciate that anything that receives enough time and attention will at least push out a little leaf and flower. (Except for my map-reading skills, which have always been a barren wasteland no matter how hard I try.)

Because this strategy of extreme performance exertion proved so successful, I repeated it in every aspect of my life for many, many years. It enabled me to launch and sustain my own business, buy my own house, and even create enough margin to pursue my true calling: writing poems, books, essays, stories, and innumerable thank-you notes on the side. I have even had the incredible privilege of working from home while raising my son.

Yet, while it's true that this mode of extreme performance contributed to many accomplishments, it often cost me the proper nourishment of a balanced life. But even more significantly, it reinforced the illusion that if I just worked harder, I could fix it—whatever it may be. And this attitude kept me very busy striving to fix things, some of which were beyond repair or maybe not even worth my time to fix.

Paradoxically, by trying so hard to make things better, I would often actually cement the state of brokenness.

Let me give you an example. For years and years, I would sit at my desk and push-push-push to figure out how to solve some problem in a piece of writing. Finally I would get up to pour a fresh cup of tea, look for the mail, pet a cat, and *BAM*: The solution presented itself as if it had been waiting all day for the opportunity to come through. All it needed was a little breathing room to find its own way.

Did this event teach me to trust ease? No way. Not for at least a decade. It took thousands of similar scenarios—in which I attempted to force a solution that could not be reached by force, only to find that the issues would simply, mysteriously work themselves out when left alone—for the cartoon light bulb to finally appear over my head. *Duh*, it said. *You made this ten times harder than it had to be. Can we stop this silliness now?*

I'm not telling you not to work hard. But I am saying that when you make any part of your writing life harder than it has to be, you're not serving yourself, your work, or your readers.

When I started releasing my compulsion to "fix," I stumbled upon a far more revolutionary approach. Often I don't engage at all with what's not working. Instead, I live in rapture with what *is* working, thereby generating more of what works. This practice has slowly anchored in me an absolute optimism and faith that I always have something solid to fall back on in my writing life.

In case there's anyone out there who's not yet a believer, I'm here to report from the other side that rapture is a far more enjoyable experience than the "have-not" frame of mind. And counting your good fortune is a whole lot more exhilarating than counting your losses.

I don't know how or why this works, but I have lived this phenomenon enough times now to know that the stuff that's not working somehow unwrinkles itself in the background when I refuse to feed it with my upset.

When you get stuck next time, or any time, consider this possibility: If it can be fixed quickly and relatively easily, it's fixable. If it can't, move on. By not engaging with a problem for a time, you may find that it is far simpler to fix it a little later. And if it's never solved, so be it. With all of the time and energy you have freed in surrendering this particular struggle, you will likely solve at least ten other, far more fixable problems.

BE FIERCE

What surprising paradoxes have you discovered as you explore the contradictions between hard work and ease? What happens when you live in rapture with what is working? How are you already doing this in your writing life? And how will you do it more?

BUILD A CATHEDRAL

In one of my favorite allegories, a traveler in medieval times comes upon a stonemason at work. He asks, "What are you doing?" The man looks weary and unhappy. He responds, "Can't you see I am cutting and laying down stone? My back is killing me, and I can't wait to stop."

The traveler continues on his way and comes upon a second stonemason. "What are you doing?" he asks. "I'm building a wall," says the stonemason. "I'm grateful to have this work so I can support my family."

As the traveler walks on, he encounters a third stonemason who seems to be doing exactly the same work as the previous two. He asks the man, "What are you doing?" The man stands up straight. His face is radiant. He looks up at the sky and spreads his arms wide. "I am building a cathedral," he answers.

All three workers are technically doing the same work: laying the stones of an edifice. But the story they tell themselves and this traveler about their labor shapes how they feel—and most likely the quality of their work.

Which stonemason are you?

Are you the first laborer, producing writing fueled by a sense of drudgery and defeat, perhaps focused on praise or publishing or competition or envy, and discouraged by how slow the process is, or how intermittent the affirmation along the way?

Are you the second laborer, focused on doing quality work and appreciative of the evolution of your craft and results?

Or, like the third stonemason, do you have a vision so compelling, so meaningful, that it fills you with a sense of joy and purpose to show up at the blank page day after day as you do the righteous work of erecting your cathedral?

You are in charge of how you work, how you think and feel about your work, and the vision you hold for where you are headed. Cathedrals hand rendered of stone are not built overnight. They are constructed collaboratively by highly skilled and practiced people over long periods of time.

If you'd like a writing life that helps you build a cathedral, consider these practices to keep you invigorated for the journey ahead.

DEFINE YOUR GOALS

Know with absolute precision what you're striving for. If you are like the second stonemason, your goal might be to produce a complete poetry collection by the end of the year, a polished pitch for an agent for the upcoming writing conference, a first-draft story to bring to the next writing group session, or a new essay to submit to a writing contest prior to the deadline.

CULTIVATE YOUR VISION

If you are like the third stonemason, you might hold the same exact goals as above but imbue them with a sense of how they contribute to erecting your cathedral. For instance, in fulfilling one or more of your goals, you might gain mastery of your craft; give service to your audience by providing the entertainment, insight, or information they want; make a meaningful and lasting contribution to the literary work in your genre; or change the global conversation about your area of expertise.

See how you lifted your eyes a little higher into the sky as you considered how the short-term goals fulfill the long-term vision?

SHOW UP AND THROW YOUR BACK INTO IT

I can't tell you how many "writers" I have encountered who are so dazzled by their vision of the cathedral that they haven't yet learned to cut or lay stone. Where vision meets sweat equity, the possibility of a cathedral is born. The third stonemason wasn't drinking a latte and relaxing in the shade as he contemplated his future cathedral. He was *in action,* laying stones that would transform his vision to edifice. We writers must do the same.

CELEBRATE LIKE YOUR WRITING DEPENDS ON IT (BECAUSE IT DOES)

When you are clear about your goals, it is far easier to evaluate whether or not you are moving toward them. The more you can appreciate the opportunities, obstacles, and successes along the way, the more you will anchor your reliability to yourself—and your satisfaction. Try these suggestions:

- **THANK EVERYONE WHO HELPS YOU**. And I mean everyone. Whether it's a weekend workshop leader, an editor who chooses (or rejects) your work, a person in your writing group who gave valuable feedback, or a writer you've never met whose essay moved you, appreciation of others is jet fuel for your own process.
- **STUDY AND REPEAT WHAT WORKS**. Make note of every little thing you do that helps move you toward your goal so that you know what to repeat the next time you have a similar goal. I keep a list of what went right every week. This helps me see the big picture of the small steps I've taken over time to create big results.
- **KEEP A CURRENT LIST AND CLIPS (OR COPIES OR A LINK) OF YOUR PUBLICATIONS**. Record the publication name, the date, and name of your piece. Update it regularly, and appreciate yourself anew each time you revisit and add to the list.
- **CLEAR A HIGHLY VISIBLE BOOKSHELF AND PUT ONLY YOUR PUBLISHED WORK ON IT**. Even if you don't have published work to shelve there yet, you are making the space and creating the invitation for it to arrive. Consider putting something beautiful and symbolic in the empty space that represents the cathedral you intend to materialize.
- **UPDATE YOUR LITERARY BIOGRAPHY QUARTERLY WITH YOUR LATEST ACCOMPLISHMENTS**. Apply this fresh version to your blog, website, and social media, as well as to your submission materials. Honor the growth of your expertise, experience, and confidence over time.

- **TUNE INTO WHAT YOU ALREADY HAVE.** When you find yourself yearning for a writing skill or habit or opportunity that you believe would make your writing process or results more effective, notice how you already have it (or some similar version of it) or are on your way to getting there. Let's say you want to improve some aspect of your craft. Chances are good you've been attending to this desire in different ways over time. Perhaps you took a workshop to help tackle this last January and read a book about it several years ago. Dig up your notes from that time. See how proficient you've become since then. If you want to be more reliable about your own deadlines, appreciate how capable you are at honoring the deadlines of others. Leverage a strength you already have to help yourself get even stronger.
- **FILE YOUR REJECTIONS IN AN "I AM BRAVE" FOLDER.** The fatter it gets, the braver you are.
- **SHARE YOUR GOOD NEWS.** Mothers can be great listeners for this. So can partners, friends, writing groups, and social networks. Success is inspiring and motivating. When you make yours visible, you unveil possibilities for the people around you.
- **CELEBRATE OTHERS' GOOD NEWS.** The delight you take in others' successes can overflow into your own sense of possibility and progress. If another person has done it, you know it's possible.

When you clearly articulate your vision and commit to cathedral-building practices, your greatest desires will begin to feel within reach.

BE FIERCE

Are you cutting stone, building a wall, or erecting a cathedral in your writing life? Which of the three stonemasons do you intend to be? The story you tell yourself—and others—makes all the difference.

YOU'RE WORTH IT

THERE ARE NO PREREQUISITES TO WORTHINESS.
—Brené Brown

My seven-year-old son, Theo, walked into the kitchen as I was preparing breakfast and asked me to play a song he'd heard at camp called "Worth It" by Fifth Harmony, which happens to be a song I dance to in Zumba every week. I looked it up online, and as the video blasted on my computer, we started shouting, "Baby, I'm worth it," and dancing wildly.

Because we have a high threshold for repetition and a limited repertoire of songs that interest us both, we played the song again. And again. And again. Most mornings now, one of us suggests we listen to it, I click *play*, and Theo and I have a spontaneous dance party in the kitchen. Through this full-body practice of joyfully insisting we're worth it, I am starting to wonder if we have actually been singing ourselves into a deeper embodiment of worthiness.

I wish this song had existed earlier in my life when I was an approval addict. Back then, I dedicated my life to seeking evidence of my worth and striving to earn it through extraordinary effort in the realm of work, family, and friendship. This effort was a lot like trying to plant potatoes on a bridge. As I'd put my sense of worth in the hands and eyes of the people around me and judged my self-value through their approval, it was impossible to harvest anything sustainable from the ever-changing ground of their opinions.

At some point I noticed my cats had a different approach.

A cat will get in your lap, demand to be petted, love you passionately for five minutes, and then dismiss you in favor of a stripe of sun on the carpet, where he will lick his belly. A cat doesn't worry if you're in the mood to pet him or how you'll feel when he's ready to move on. He's clear about his desire, unquestioning of his worthiness, and certain that you exist as some sort of cozy, semi-comprehensible, desire-fulfilling ecosystem. In fact, my cat, Diablo, is so at one with his certainty that he is deserving of attention that he will generously pet himself with any body part of mine sticking out from the covers while I sleep.

Marie Forleo has been a powerful teacher for me as I've worked on manifesting what I desire. She asks, "How would you act if you were the best in the world at what you do?" I love this question because it challenges me to take myself seriously. But lately I am starting to think there is an imperative question that precedes this one, and if we don't ask and answer it for ourselves before asking this one, it can become the bottleneck in our process, our joy, and our results.

This question is: How would you act if you were sure you deserved the writing life you want? If you don't feel worthy, it doesn't matter how many great productivity strategies you've tried. It doesn't matter how many followers or likes or subscribers you have. It doesn't matter how many publication notches you have on your belt—or how celebrated you are. One need only look at the ample evidence in the realm of celebrity tragedy to realize that being the best at something doesn't necessarily ensure or reflect a positive sense of self.

When I heard Charles Eisenstein speak recently, he pointed out that we didn't earn being born, didn't earn our parents' care and nurturing, didn't earn the soil, the water we drink, or the sun. We didn't even earn our own capacity to work hard. We simply showed up here on earth, and these gifts were given to us.

As he spoke, I realized that so many of us burn unnecessary rubber trying to earn the gifts we have already been given, instead of simply appreciating them—and through that appreciation, cementing the certainty of our worthiness.

I have come to see gratitude as a kind of enzyme that lets us digest the banquet of our lives, our desires, and our accomplishments. Once you have found a way to tolerate, or even enjoy, the good work you are doing and the good results you are manifesting, then you can begin to consider and reach toward being extraordinary at what you do.

Gratitude changes your inner conversation from wondering if you deserve to have what you want to simply noticing and appreciating all you have already been given. From that place of abundance, you will be far more receptive to what you are striving to create, such that you'll come to see worth as something you learn to embody, not something you earn.

Paradoxically, appreciating what you have already is how you teach yourself that you deserve to have it—and so much more.

BE FIERCE

How would you act if you believed there were no prerequisites to worthiness?

MAKE IT MATTER

When I worked as a senior copywriter at a marketing agency, the campaigns I worked on often were re-imagined and re-created fifteen or more times before going live. Every now and then, a campaign wouldn't go live at all. While this outcome demoralized some of my colleagues, I did not share their discouragement.

For me, writing is an end unto itself; the practice is my reward. Refining a piece of writing in search of the right way to express an idea is endlessly satisfying to me. Each time I was asked for something different, I welcomed the new challenge.

As the clients and creative team sorted out their priorities, I stayed focused on the fact that every draft I wrote mattered—to me, at least. Eventually, I understood that it was my commitment to "make it matter" that kept my head above the subjective waters of agency life. By the time the client signed off on the campaign, I'd advanced my writing practice through the discipline of meeting their needs.

Because I put my emphasis on the writing process (versus the end product), I was not so emotionally dependent on its results. Therefore, every step I took toward improvement was enjoyable.

But let me be clear: I was obsessed about doing exceptional work. I'd stay up all night iterating concepts. I'd bolt up out of a dead sleep to write down taglines and calls to action. I'd get so lost in generative thought that I'd arrive at work with no memory of the transit there. During a weeklong, flu-induced delirium, I was plagued with nightmares about the television show *Mad Men*, in which I tried to repair Don Draper's flailing cigarette campaign. Each time I woke up in a sweat, I reminded myself that I wasn't Peggy and that Don wasn't actually counting on me to solve anything for him.

In short, I made my agency work matter. I was well aware that becoming a more strategic and creative copywriter not only served my employer, my creative team, and our clients, but also uplifted my poetry, my essays, and my fiction. As my language grew more compelling, more precise, and more unexpected, I refined myself to a pencil point through collaboration with some extraordinarily talented people.

You can take whatever life gives you, from your job to your dog to your heartbreak to your addiction, and make it matter to your writing life. We all have proof of this on our bookshelves. Anna Sam turned the vile behavior of her grocery store checkout customers into a huge international bestseller, *Checkout.* Cheryl Strayed (*Wild*) and Ariel Gore (*The End of Eve*) took two very different paths as they navigated the loss of their mothers through memoir. Elizabeth Gilbert transformed her divorce into redemption in *Eat, Pray, Love.*

Every struggle, loss, joy, discovery, inconvenience, heartbreak, awkward moment, and feeling of sheer terror can inform your writing life.

Whatever life presents you, if you commit to making it matter, you can elevate your experience to inform your art. Because life has presented me with Twitter, I have been experimenting with ways to make it matter. At a recent conference, instead of taking notes on my computer during the keynote lecture as I typically do, I decided to tweet about what I was learning instead. Metabolizing big ideas in miniscule character counts turned out to be a pretty interesting way to learn. And by simultaneously sending something out (in the form of a tweet) that I was also taking in, I felt a higher responsibility for the information.

As I tweeted nuggets of insight that were meaningful to me, with an ear for how they might be useful to other readers interested in the topic, I realized that live tweeting was an exercise in micro speed-publishing—instantaneous reporting. A marketer by day, I also was gratified by using hashtags that would link my tweet to both the speaker and the conference. I was helping their ideas gain visibility and momentum by declaring to the Twitterverse that they mattered to me.

But I didn't stop there. In the TweetDeck column I created for the conference hashtag, I watched as numerous live tweets accumulated. I traveled deeper into the material I was hearing through the reflections of other participants who were also tweeting about it. As we shared our thoughts and responses to the material, we were not just listeners taking in a great presentation; we were contributing to the conversation in real time. I was hooked.

By deciding that Twitter mattered, I taught myself a new mode of engagement that truly delighted me. And by increasing my accountability with tweets, I entered the conversation in a new way. As a result, Twitter has become an important social channel in the realms where I work and play.

BE FIERCE

What technology platform or work conundrum or family drama could be of benefit if you make it matter to your writing life? How could you lean in to these moments—and, in so doing, gain fresh insight? How could this introduce you to a new capacity or commitment in yourself that you didn't know you were ready to bring forward? How might you transform challenge or boredom or disinterest into opportunity by simply shining your writerly light of inquiry?

TO PLAN IS HUMAN; TO SCHEDULE IS DIVINE

DON'T PRIORITIZE YOUR SCHEDULE. SCHEDULE YOUR PRIORITIES.
—Steven Covey

In a webinar I was teaching, a student asked: "I have twelve projects in the works, and they're all of equal priority. How do I know what I should do first?"

I responded, "That's what the middle of the night is for!"

I was taking lightly what is a rather serious concern for so many of us. When you don't know what's most important, you can't prioritize how to spend your time, you don't know when you've met your goals, and you can literally end up working through the night—usually on the wrong project.

In contrast, when you know what you want, you can get it—systematically, deliberately, over time. And you can evaluate your effectiveness as you go.

A highly effective and accomplished mentor of mine once said that if he had five days left to live, he'd spend the first two days planning to make sure he spent the last three days of his life exactly the way he wanted. This made an impression on me.

You might be in such a hurry, in such a state of overwhelm, that you can't see an alternative to your habit of reactivity. Whatever is loudest or most uncomfortable or most important to someone else gets your attention first, and thus you remain in a cycle of doing instead of planning. Eventually this cycle becomes a downward spiral. You end up stuck, exhausted, and convinced that you're not capable of achieving work that matters to you.

Whereas, when you align your work with your priorities, it's like turning a screw into a stud instead of into drywall. You give the enormous effort of your writing a strong and sure foothold. And you give yourself a meaningful sense of clarity and direction.

When you're ready to stop writing through the night and hoping you chose the right piece to focus on, I suggest that you try planning.

If, like my student, you have twelve projects that have equal priority, start by narrowing your list to the top three. Research suggests that too many choices can immobilize you. Having just a few choices, on the other hand, helps you clarify your priorities and be more effective in your decision making. I experienced this firsthand when I judged a poetry contest a few years ago. I had to select from approximately three thousand submissions the top twenty poems in order of merit. I found it far easier to identify the top three poems than to distinguish between which poems deserved to be ranked eighth or eighteenth. Having so many poems to consider and order at once was simply overwhelming.

You can keep those other nine items in your to-do list on the backburner and advance them to the top of your list once you've crossed off the top three projects. Or you can even swap items on your list as you go, as your projects and priorities change.

Not sure how to prioritize? Start by weighing what you value most in a project's completion. Will one project be easier to finish and therefore give you a sense of much-needed momentum? Is one due tomorrow to a client or publication? Would one be more fun? Does one need to rest for a while as you work on something else? Trust your instincts as you quickly make that list, and then start with the first one. You can always reshuffle priorities later if you need to. The most important thing is to start with what matters most—and keep going.

ENTER THE MIGHTY SCHEDULE

A schedule is the closest thing we realists have to a crystal ball. It helps us envision our future by mapping out the path to getting there. If you owe a manuscript to your publisher in six months, for example, you can determine which hours on which days of every week you intend to write, and reserve the time. As you plug in the hours you intend to work, you may discover that you'll likely meet your deadline two months early— or that you'll need more time, so you'll have to demote another priority that is currently taking time away from your book.

On my computer calendar, I designate a different color for each of my priorities so I can see at a glance the mix of personal commitments, client work deadlines, and designated writing time for any given day. Within my writing time blocks, my schedule indicates which of my many writing priorities I plan to work on.

I think of my schedule as a promise I make to myself and to everyone counting on me. I commit to myself in blocks of color: At a glance, I can see that I will drive my son, Theo, to school from 7:15 to 8:00. I will take the dog to her rehab appointment from 9:00 to 10:00. I will complete the client project from 10:00 to 3:30. I will collect Theo from school at 4:00. And from 8:30 to 10:00 in the evening, when he is asleep, I will work on my top-priority writing project. I can scan through the week and see that on Saturday from 9:00 A.M. to noon, I'm scheduled to work on my priority number two writing project, and I am relieved that this work is accounted for.

In this way, my commitments to myself become as natural and absolute as my commitments to everyone else. My inner voice of protest doesn't get a say when it's time to drive to the orthodontist. Nor does it get a say when it's time to sit down and write a chapter.

When you know what you want, and you know that you have scheduled the time you need to achieve it, you can minimize your inner overwhelm and create the best possible conditions for calm, clear, focused work that takes you where you want to go.

HONOR YOUR LINEAGE

I have always been magnetically drawn to the books I need as teachers. Recently I cleared a shelf and, with great reverence, placed on it the books I most love—the ones that have shaped me in the way that water shapes stones, almost imperceptibly over time.

Whenever I scan their proud spines all lined up in a row, I think of how this shelf reflects my literary lineage. These are the poets and writers whose work whispers directly into my ear to penetrate my being and reveal what I need to know about being a person and a writer. These are my literary ancestors and immediate family.

I consider each book with gratitude: Sharon Olds's *The Dead and the Living*, the dog-eared, tear-stained poetry collection that I have been returning to since my early twenties when I so desperately wanted to write a collection of its caliber that I considered giving up poetry altogether; Lidia Yuknavitch's *The Chronology of Water: A Memoir*, which sings through me as if its narrative were a plucked string of the sitar calling forth my own story in accompaniment; Kim Rosen's *Saved By a Poem*, affirming my lifelong practice of poetry as sacred medicine; *When Things Fall Apart*, by Pema Chódrón, which has instructed me how to make the crossing from resistance to acceptance in my darkest moments.

This small literary collection, along with the rest of the books on my "lineage shelf" is a funhouse mirror reflection of who I am, what I love, and from where I have come. I imagine the little serif font letters swimming through my cells. The words that come through me now have breathed the amniotic suspended dreams of every word I have admired, allowed in, and sent back into the world. These titles are a bouquet harvested of my desire to enter the universal human experience through poem and story.

Here, in the authority and stability of its literary family, the title of my next project presents itself. It is shy, wobbly, unsure of whether to trust my hand. We sit together, and I listen. Take a few notes. A large fluff of dandelion seed drifts by my open window as the peas in the garden bed below nod in the wind.

By taking the time to name and appreciate my literary lineage, the next step on my path reveals itself to me. I wonder if that's really all our writing asks of us: to know what we love, to listen, and to give ourselves over to what presents itself.

BE FIERCE

I invite you to honor the books you love most by giving them their own shelf (or even their own pile). Then sit with them and appreciate how they have informed your vision, your craft, or your sense of direction in your writing life. Is something inside you lingering on the peripheries, wanting to come through? What work of yours belongs on this shelf, in this company? What knowledge have you gained from these books that now informs your own literary legacy?

MASTER THE MARGIN

I was talking to a client of mine—a naturopath—about how he was going to make time to do some of the marketing writing assignments I'd given him. He was considering seeing patients one less day a week so he could set aside a stretch of time for writing. But this seemed at odds with his goal of growing his business, which was why he was tackling these writing assignments in the first place.

I asked him if he ever had any down time between seeing patients. He thought about this and realized that though some days were entirely full, on many others he had anywhere from forty-five minutes to two hours of free time before the next appointment. I challenged him to sit down during every in-between time and do his homework then. I explained that he might actually find it easier to tackle this work in small chunks throughout the week. Sometimes a big chunk of time can overwhelm us and shut us down.

I know from working with writers and working with myself for the past twenty years that it's easy to waste a full day that you've set aside for writing. It can be less intimidating to fit your writing time into the margins you already have. This can help you get a foothold into those wider expanses of time, should you be so fortunate to eventually create such opportunities.

I suppose what I'm saying is that I've come to see the sour grapes of being so busy as an opportunity for making wine. I believe that what most writers struggle with—fitting their projects into small slivers of time—can actually be an efficient way to piece together the whole pie.

The less time you have, the more compelled you will often be to make every minute count.

Not sure this could work for you? I have a few suggestions:

1. **USE WAITING TIME AS WRITING TIME**. Standing in line? Made it early to your appointment? Kids delayed after school? Keep a notebook and pen handy, and take the opportunity to write while you wait.

2. **EMBRACE INSOMNIA**. Barbara Kingsolver wrote her first book entirely in the middle of the night while suffering from pregnancy-induced insomnia. I did, too. I'm not recommending sleeplessness as a life strategy, but when insomnia strikes, it might be because you have something important to say that's trying to come through. Or it could be because you're pregnant. But that's another story.

3. **LOVE THE LULLS**. No matter how hard you work at your job, there are always spaces in between the work. Whether it's during a lunch break, on your morning or evening commute, or while the computers are down for ten minutes, use those minutes to squeeze in some writing.

4. **SET THE ALARM FIFTEEN MINUTES EARLIER**. Yep, that's it. Just fifteen minutes. Write like mad before you do anything else.

5. **QUIT SOMETHING**. Whether it's a committee, a regular social hour, or a time-consuming household chore that someone else could do, renegotiate that commitment. Put yourself first. Use those two hours a week to write.

6. **MAKE THE MINDLESS TASKS MINDFUL**. I have been walking dogs for the past seventeen years. I might consider this task a drain on my writing life, but instead it has become my most precious idea-generation time. The ideas and images that bubble up as I walk with my canine companions grow into blog posts, poems, classes, books. When you're in the shower, washing dishes, or on the treadmill at the gym, pay attention to what moves through you. And make sure you write it down!

7. **ASK YOUR SUBCONSCIOUS TO SOLVE IT**. Even when you don't have a sliver of time to write, you may have a bit of available attention to devote to your writing process. Before going to sleep or setting off on your commute, try asking something specific of your subconscious. Are you struggling with a particular metaphor? Is a snippet of dialogue refusing to sing? Are you devoid of fresh ideas? You may be surprised by how much you can solve before returning to the page.

8. **BABY YOUR WRITING**. When a baby cries, you don't tell her, "I promised so-and-so I'd do such-and-such. I'll be with you in about fifteen

minutes." You drop what you're doing, figure out what the baby needs, and then give it to her. What if you gave your writing the same attention? What if you sprinted toward an index card every time a powerful image or phrase or snippet of dialogue presented itself, and then you took thirty seconds to get the words down, no matter how inconvenient it might be?

9. **BE FAITHFUL TO YOUR MUSE.** This tip completes the thought I started in the point above. Once you're confident that you can count on yourself to take note of what's coming through (and your muse shares your confidence), ideas and inspiration will flow more freely.

10. **APPRECIATE YOURSELF.** No one but you will know how hard you're working to carve out writing space. So it's your job to appreciate every sliver of writing time you claim for yourself. Make a chart and give yourself stars, take yourself out for a drink, call your mother and brag—whatever works for you. Just make sure you find some way to take a step back and say, "Hey! My actions are in line with my values! I'm discovering ways to write in life's margins on a regular basis! I can count on myself to get writing done!"

Mastering the margin can make the difference between writing and not writing—and it can give you real momentum toward reaching your goals.

BE FIERCE

I showed you mine—now show me yours! Go to fierceonthepage.com/masterthemargin to share three of your best tips for microwriting with our community of fierce writers and see what's working for your peers as well.

CHANGE YOURSELF

WHEN WE ARE NO LONGER ABLE TO CHANGE A SITUATION, WE ARE CHALLENGED TO CHANGE OURSELVES. —*Viktor E. Frankl*

Being self-employed for nearly two decades has taught me accountability. When things go wrong, I can't blame anyone else for my mistakes or ask them to shield me from the consequences. Because I am solely responsible for what's working and not working, I strive to quickly learn, adapt, and grow through any difficulty.

This accountability has also served me well in my writing life. When I am not succeeding as I intended, I look for ways I am influencing the unwanted outcome rather than blaming the person or publication or situation that disappointed me. And when things go right, I pay close attention to the choices that led me there—so I can repeat them.

This attention to my process and results gives me agency to steer more coherently in the direction I want to go. By honoring my successes, accepting responsibility for my missteps, and continuing to explore options to course-correct, I am standing in my authority to create the writing life I want.

Endless variables that we can't control will always be a part of life, writing, and publishing. But you *can* change yourself by taking responsibility for your evolution. How can you prepare yourself to be receptive to the results you want? And how can you respond responsibly when things don't work out, without losing heart or momentum? Here are some of my best ideas.

COMMIT YOURSELF

William Hutchinson Murray advises:

> … the moment one definitely commits oneself, then Providence moves too. All sorts of things occur to help one that would never otherwise have occurred. A whole stream of events issues from the decision, raising in one's favor all manner of unforeseen incidents and meetings and material assistance, which no man could have dreamed would have come his way. Whatever you can do, or dream you can do, begin it. Boldness has genius, power, and magic in it. Begin it now.

Anything you commit to in your writing life is possible to achieve. It might not happen quickly or easily or the way you expect it to, but you are the author of your writing life, and you are in charge of its beginning, middle, and end. Simply planting both feet on the ground of your desire and declaring your commitment to yourself and to the people who care about you is one of the most powerful actions you can take to align yourself with that goal.

When I think of commitment, I see the inflated punching bag my brother and I played with as kids. This clown-shaped toy, which was as tall as we were, was weighted at the bottom and impossible to topple. We'd hit it, and it would tip backwards briefly and then quickly right itself. Commitment has this same mingling of lightness and gravitas. When you are blown back, simply straighten up and keep going.

DECLARE IT AWESOME IN ADVANCE

When my son, Theo, was two, he and I had a ritual of shouting, "AWESOME NAP!" before each nap to set our shared expectation as he settled into bed. You have the same option to set the level of awesomeness every time you sit down at your desk or send out a submission. You can simply choose, at any moment, with no direct cause and effect, to be thrilled with your writing life. You can declare it an AWESOME SUBMISSION or decide it will be an AWESOME WRITING SESSION—and then make it so.

INVITE YOUR RESISTANCE TO TEA

There is much truth in the old adage, "What you resist, persists." As a writer you must find ways to be curious about and friendly toward your resistance so that you can ultimately relax and even disarm it. When you ask your resistance to pull up a chair at the kitchen table and tell you its story, you gain insight about where you are vulnerable, what you're trying to protect, and how you can accept this tender part of yourself. Once resistance has a chance to air its concerns fully, it stops struggling and settles back among the Greek chorus of advisors at your personal executive table. And you'll be able to proceed unimpeded.

CONSIDER IT ALL INSTRUCTION

Life is a learning laboratory. When you strive toward a goal and don't reach it, you can redirect the disappointment toward insight with a little effort. Once you're done licking your wounds, it's time to seek out instruction. What worked? What didn't? Where are you already strong? Where do you need more practice, education, or resources? How will you proceed from here? The more you relentlessly seek out ways to learn from your losses, the more effectively you'll refine yourself into a writer who knows how to find her way through any obstacle in pursuit of her goals and dreams.

MAKE IT A SUCCESS

You get to decide what success means in your writing life, and I think we all benefit from setting the bar quite low. If winning the National Book Award is your only measure for success, you are missing out on endless opportunities to appreciate yourself and enjoy your many triumphs along the way.

I propose that setting a goal to complete a piece of writing is a success. And showing up at your desk to write when you say you will is a success. And attending the reading that fills you with fresh ideas about language and image is a success. Leaning into those four rounds of revision is a success. Researching publications where you'd like to be published is a success. And then taking the risk to submit your work to those publications is a success. Those are six successes that precede the news of publication or rejection. And they can't be taken away from you, no matter what happens next.

• • •

Until you get the result you want for your writing, keep experimenting with changes—to your approach and attitude. When you take responsibility for learning, adapting, celebrating, and finding your way forward, no matter what, you will discover the channel to your genius, power, and magic.

DEFINE SUCCESS ON YOUR TERMS

Success means different things to each of us at each stage of our writing life. Early in my poetry-writing days, just showing a poem to someone was triumph—and that took me a decade. In later years, standing up in front of an audience to read my poems (and surviving) became my measure of success.

Back then, writing was as imperative to me as breathing, and I didn't need to set goals about the writing itself. But my terror of making my inner world "outer" was so extreme that all of my success energy centered around talking down my fears. To this day, I still work with my fear of visibility in my ever-increasing public life. It took years to settle into telling the truth on my various blogs. In fact, social media has stretched my visibility fears and related success standards in some pretty interesting directions.

In different seasons of my writing career, the success standards have been quite different. I wanted dual careers, with enough space in my professional life to devote to my unpaid writing. I wanted to write and publish books. I wanted give back to writers by teaching, coaching, and editing. Then I wanted to write less so I had more time for my new family. Then I wanted to write poems as transportation through my divorce. And so on. Each of these desires and goals had a success standard baked in. Some of these standards were internal, like showing up at the page at incredibly inconvenient times, and some were external, like being willing to stand in the shoes of an expert, flaws and all.

Often writers focus so completely on a long-term goal that we forget to define the road markers of success along the way. For example, it's wonderful to intend to be a famous novelist and hold that big sun up over your journey. And it's even more wonderful if you have an idea of what your next success should be along the way. Maybe it's showing up at your writing desk two hours a day, or taking that class that's going to help you better understand character development, or saying no to someone you're in the habit of saying yes to. I think all of us need a mix of those "someday" and "right now" success benchmarks to keep us striving, as well as satisfied, with what we are able to accomplish in any given moment.

I think of it like this: Each time a success becomes built in as practice, it's time to set your sights on the next one. And there are no time constraints for this. As I mentioned, I've spent decades on a few of my writing goals. You'll discover your own speed bumps and open roads as you go. It doesn't matter what anyone else is doing, or at what speed.

Pace yourself. Honor yourself. Be willing to define and redefine success from moment to moment, week to week, year to year. It's your writing life. You get to make it work the way you want.

BE FIERCE

The tricky thing about pursuing success over the long arc of a writing life is that the layers of who we are and who we have been are always reshuffling. Chances are good that we are all living by success standards we have outgrown, that someone else has set for us, or that we have unreasonably imposed on ourselves. Can you think of one such example—and then let it go? What does success mean to you today, what small accomplishments are leading you there, and how do you intend to keep moving in that direction? Tell us about it at fierceonthepage.com/successonyourterms.

TWO KEYS TO UNLOCK YOUR MOMENTUM

The world is brimming with advice about how to write more and write better. Chances are good that you've explored some—or maybe even many—of these recommendations. Chances are also good that you're not getting the kind of mileage you'd expect from adapting these approaches.

What's in your way?

Before you can make good use of someone else's advice, it's important to develop a realistic picture of who you are, what your tendencies are, and what you're realistically willing and able to change. Two key approaches can take you there.

The first is perception. You are better equipped to reach your goals when you notice with fresh and friendly eyes who you are and how you operate. Where do you stall and when do you take flight? What are you doing when you have your best ideas? How do you waste time? What writing do you admire? What do you want so badly that you haven't even articulated it yet?

So many of us are so entrenched in our unconscious ways of doing and being that we have no idea what's broken, and therefore we are not in a position to intelligently decide what needs fixing. Nor do we recognize and appreciate our gifts, our strengths, and our anchors of existing momentum. We may not even know what our true aspirations are, so we have no concrete way of striving for them or evaluating if we're reaching them.

Simply paying attention to the way you write—and don't write—can be the start of a sea change. Pretend you are an anthropologist studying the culture of you. Keep a log of observations—about the behaviors, attitudes, and habits you notice as you write. Your job is not to judge, but to get clearer about who you are as a writer.

Once you're working with an informed picture of how you write (and how you don't), the second key to unlocking your momentum is giving yourself permission to be you. That's right. Just because you read once that "serious" writers get MFAs or do manual labor to have more writing time doesn't necessarily mean you are called to do the same. Maybe most poets write only poetry, but you span multiple genres. No problem. Perhaps you think you should write faster, be less stiff in front of an audience, sharpen your pencil more often. When you know yourself well, you can let go of advice about what you should be doing and spend time doing things that actually help you succeed.

While driving the other day, I caught myself in an inner monologue, chastising myself with this odd thought: *Other people must be better at being happy than I am.* I felt like a big disappointment on the happiness-maintenance scale. Then some part of me—I like to think it's the Fierce Writer I've been cultivating all these years—interrupted this negative self-talk with the challenge: *Well, so what? Let's say that other people are actually better at being happy. What difference does that make? This is who you are. What do you intend to make of it?*

Simply knowing and welcoming yourself can help you find true and enduring momentum as you let go of the strategies and attitudes that don't fit—to make room for the ones that do.

BE FIERCE

What unfriendly things do you tell yourself that make you feel unwel-
come? I propose that you release the oppression of who you believe you
are supposed to be as a writer. No need to force yourself to do something
the "right way" if it's not your right way. Your job is to honor your process,
your rhythms, and your voice by finding ways to put them in service to
your writing life. Give yourself permission to be exactly who you are.
The welcomed writing self is far more receptive to fine-tuning systems,
habits, and craft. The paradox is that when you welcome the writer you
are today, you clear a space in which the writer you always wanted to
be can come forward.

BYOB: BECOME YOUR OWN BRAND

We often recognize business brands by their taglines, such as Nike's "Just Do It," Apple's "Think Different," and L'Oréal's "Because You're Worth It." Each brand builds a bridge between what the company offers and how the consumer wants to feel. Buying Nike products reinforces our desire to be make-it-happen people. Our Macs make a statement about our innovative thinking. And our L'Oréal makeup confirms that we're worth the attention and affirmation we seek.

WHY WRITERS NEED BRANDS

The business of writing begins where the craft of writing leaves off. Pitching to editors and publishers, promoting your work once it's been published, and sustaining relationships with readers over time are all important elements of the business of writing. This is why I propose that every writer think of herself as an entrepreneur with an easily recognizable brand that helps people anticipate the type of experience they can expect from her.

As a writer, your brand is both the promise you make about who you are, as well as how you live (and write) it. Think of the contrast between Jonathan Franzen and Jennifer Weiner—the books they write, their responses in interviews, their opinions of each other. When you buy a book by either author, you have a pretty good idea of what kind of experience to expect, right?

NAME AND CLAIM THE BRAND OF YOU

Now I'm going to ask a few questions to get you thinking about your brand, accompanied by my answers about my own brand to better illustrate each point.

- **WHO ARE YOUR READERS (OR WHO WOULD YOU LIKE YOUR READERS TO BE)?** *My readers are committed to their own evolution. They want to discover new ways to be effective, productive, and successful. And they want a relationship with an author they can trust and enjoy.*
- **WHAT ARE YOU OFFERING THEM (AND HOW WOULD YOU LIKE THEM TO SEE YOU)?** *I want to offer motivation, inspiration, and information for readers. I want them to see me as a friend accompanying them through whatever topic I'm covering—whether it be creative writing, marketing, or divorce.*
- **WHAT IS YOUR BRAND VOICE (THE TONE, LANGUAGE, AND PERSONALITY OF YOUR WRITING)?** *My voice is friendly, welcoming, encouraging, occasionally exalted, practical, and poetic.*

I learned a great deal about my brand voice when I used profanity on my Path of Possibility blog. I had been given a mug that said, "Write like a motherf#ck$r," (Cheryl Strayed's fabulous declaration from her Dear Sugar column), and I wrote a blog post about how I planned to make this my new mantra for the year.

When a few blog subscribers immediately unsubscribed with accompanying notes about how disappointed they were in my profane language, I discovered that my brand voice is far more wholesome and PG-rated than the language I might be inclined to use on occasion in my own home. I understood that it must have been a shock for some readers to see the word *motherf#ck$r* coming from an earnest helper type like me.

Often we learn the hard way about the promises we've implicitly made to readers. But as with any growing process, we can simply evaluate what needs updating and course-correct as we go. I'm not saying we should be wholesome because it's what our readers want, but that we should be aware of what we've conditioned our audience to expect and should make choices informed by this insight. If and when our public image needs some updating, we can always let readers know what they can expect from us in the future.

CHOOSE A BRAND TAGLINE

How would you sum up what your writing offers and how it connects with what the reader is seeking? This is something that you can have fun considering and then adapting as you and your readers evolve.

When my first nonfiction book was published and my sense of self as a writer was entirely poetic, my brand tagline or organizing principle was "Writing the Life Poetic," which was also the title of that first book.

When my second book was published and I had expanded my conversation with writers to include productivity, I discovered that what mattered to me most was helping people transform possibilities into probabilities. So I went public with "The Path of Possibility in Writing and in Life" (the name of my current blog for writers).

Today I've stretched the umbrella even wider to include the marketing and advertising copywriting I do for businesses and the guidance I provide for divorcing parents. I have distilled all of this, including my offerings for writers, to "Writing the Stories That Take You There."

What might your brand tagline be?

BE FIERCE

The clearer you are about what you're offering, the more powerfully you can deliver it. I'm not proposing that you need to choose a brand tagline and declare it to the world at this very moment—or ever. However, this might be a fun and useful exercise: First, consider the types of reading experiences you expect from your favorite writers. Then distill these experiences into short statements or taglines for those writers. From there, consider your own.

FIND (AND KEEP) YOUR X

LET THE BEAUTY YOU LOVE BE WHAT YOU DO. THERE ARE A THOUSAND WAYS TO KNEEL AND KISS THE EARTH. —*Rumi*

In my midtwenties I was at a bar dancing wildly to my boyfriend's band and having a really good time. A woman approached me and asked where I got my X. I though she was talking about my Swatch watch, which had a big X on the face.

"Macy's," I shouted over the music. She gave me a strange look and clarified that she wanted to know where I got my ecstasy—as in the drug. She thought I was high on it, and she wanted some.

We all have an inner X that marks the sweet spot where what we're doing becomes so effortless and enjoyable that the people around us want to get in on the action. I propose that all of your best writing comes from that place. Whether it's a topic or genre that consumes you, or a practice you have (like yoga or meditation or kite flying) that gives you a relationship with your inner world, knowing how to recognize and sustain your X can elevate your well-being and your performance.

This amusing misunderstanding about my X came to mind one blazing summer morning as my dog and I approached the water bowl my neighbors leave out daily on their front lawn. I've been walking my dogs for seventeen years now, and I've had every type of encounter imaginable with neighbors along the way. In all this time, the water bowl on the lawn was the first evidence I had seen that a family loved dogs so much that they invited them on their property and wanted them to be comfortable.

I was smiling at the closed door of the house when, as if on cue, the door opened and a buoyant couple materialized. Dick introduced himself and his wife, Mollie, and asked how my dog and I were enjoying the water. When I told him that I always marveled at how clean it was, my neighbor explained that he changed the water every two hours.

As we discussed various topics (the visitation schedule of coyotes, the largest number of passing-by dogs that he had counted in a single day—sixty-seven—and why my dog dropped and rolled in full-bodied pleasure in the same spot of his yard daily), my mind sang with this man's simple but profound practice of changing the water in his public dog bowl every two hours. So big was his love. So enormous was his concern for a neighborhood full of creatures he didn't know.

As we walked away, I vowed to "change the water every two hours" in my writing life. I would tend to what mattered with such love and care that it had no alternative but to thrive.

Dick and Mollie's ever-fresh water bowl got me thinking about the relationship between pleasure and discipline—and the places where we tend to create the most interference for ourselves.

I once thought that if whatever I was striving for wasn't difficult, it wasn't worthwhile. That slogging uphill carrying a boulder made me a good person, a worthy contributor.

Of course, difficulty and the fruits of its labors can be quite worthwhile. However, without some primary pleasure or passion or core commitment to fuel the uphill climb, we are far more likely to become bitter, exhausted, sick, and probably not very pleasant to be around.

I'd much rather be the person so gratified that I look intoxicated—so much so that other people envy my perceived drug supply—than the person who's bumming them out because she's doing work that doesn't set her on fire.

If you aren't inclined to refresh the water in your bowl every two hours, this could be a sign that you're not called to the work you thought you were. If people aren't stopping you in the street to ask you about it, if it's not waking you up at 4 A.M. with a barrage of ideas and insights, maybe it's not your priority right now—which can be quite useful to know. When you're not in your X zone, I invite you to simply put aside what doesn't obsess you and look for something that does—even if it's not convenient. Even if it's not what you had in mind. When you follow your X, you maximize your energy and your impact. The momentum you receive can elevate every other contribution you make, just as a rising tide lifts all boats.

LET IT GO, LET IT GO

THERE IS AN UNSEEN LIFE THAT DREAMS US. IT KNOWS OUR TRUE DIRECTION AND DESTINY. WE CAN TRUST OURSELVES MORE THAN WE REALIZE, AND WE NEED HAVE NO FEAR OF CHANGE.
— John O'Donahue

If you have a child or know a child, chances are good that the song "Let It Go" from the Disney film *Frozen* has taken up residence in your central nervous system. I, too, have not been immune.

Somehow, through its many repetitions, the song went from being enjoyable to irritating to a path of inquiry. I read a book on happiness. I read a book on tidying. I consulted a feng shui expert. All of my explorations led to a single thesis statement: It was time to let go of all that was no longer serving me.

I cleared files, furniture, and books in my office; eliminated a backlog of eight thousand unread e-mails; got rid of every single piece of clothing that did not thrill or fit me; systematized twenty years of writing in my Dropbox folders; purged twelve years of largely unexamined stuff in my freezer and medicine cabinet; and brought Theo's room entirely up to date with only the clothing, books, and toys he currently used.

The impact was dramatic. I felt light, energized, and unburdened of old stories, relationships, and interpretations of myself that no longer fit. I was literally tingling with possibility.

And in those freshly ordered drawers, spacious closets, shelves with room for new interests, and rooms liberated from the expired detritus of the past, seeds began to stir beneath the surface of my life. Client work poured in. I completed a book proposal that had been languishing for several years—then quickly pitched and sold it. I got ahead of my finances and my calendar with clear intention and execution for the first time in nearly a decade—such that I was putting my house back in order (literally and figuratively) in ways I hadn't imagined possible.

Without the weight of unaddressed clutter pressing in from the shadows of my life, I was able to think, plan, create, and execute much more clearly and effectively. So much so that the art of letting go has become my most effective productivity strategy. Let's explore some ways that it can become yours, too.

MAKE ROOM FOR WHAT YOU WANT

The most important outcome of letting go of the old is clearing the way for the new to take shape.

Giving away the clothing I'd saved for twenty-five years helped me fully embrace my age and size as I am right now. Paradoxically, the less I expected myself to be that extremely out-of-date interpretation of myself, the more fit I became and youthful I felt.

I discovered that equally important to clearing space is filling the void intentionally with what you want next. Slowly I accumulated a wardrobe that reflected middle-aged-mother-writer-entrepreneur me. In my writing life, too, as the distractions of my in-box, filing system, and bookshelf cleared, my vision clarified and I was able to align my daily choices more coherently with my long-term goals.

REORIENT YOURSELF

In feng shui terms, just choosing the right place for your desk can totally change the game. It changed mine. My desk, like most people's, was against a wall. When I sat at it, my back was to the room's door. I learned that this created the feeling of being up against a wall with no room to expand, and of being vulnerable to what was approaching from behind.

I moved my desk to the middle of the room, with one side against the wall, so that I now look out into my office and face the door to the room. This new position feels extremely different—like I'm in the command center looking out on possibility, instead of tucked away in an isolated corner.

I also distilled my hodgepodge of furniture to a single unit that matches and faces my desk—giving me a sense of visual unity. Every time I look up from my screen, I see the books I've written, the books that have been most important to me, the books I am learning from now, photos of my son and presents he has made me, and other symbolic items that fill me with joy and possibility.

It may be coincidence that my new sense of spaciousness, beauty, and continuity happened to coincide with one of the most prolific and prosperous times in my career. Or it could be that aligning my physical space was a declaration of alignment that resounded through other dimensions of my life. I encourage you to try it and see for yourself.

VOTE THEM OFF THE ISLAND

When you enter a romantic relationship, you are aware that it may possibly end. But you often expect other types of relationships to endure forever. Some do—and should. And others are more like the clothes you've been saving since college—they stopped fitting a long time ago. When you acknowledge this to yourself, you have choices about how to proceed. In reality shows, people get voted off islands, but in reality, you get to choose in less spectacular ways who belongs in your inner circle and who doesn't. If there are people in your writing life whose presence doesn't fundamentally contribute to your well-being or the forward momentum of your work, you may want to consider reducing or eliminating such input. This creates space for more appropriate friends, colleagues, and teachers to enter.

LET GO OF SOMETHING YOU THINK YOU NEED TO SUCCEED

Once I thought I needed an office in my home and the identity of the self-employed entrepreneur in order to write. Maybe I needed those things at one time, but eventually I realized that I was just in the habit of believing them to be necessary. When I spontaneously let them go to become an employee at a marketing agency for a few years, it felt liberating to stretch into a new mode of creation and collaboration outside of my home. What do you think you need that you can actually let go of, and how might doing so give you more of what you actually need?

DREAM INTO THE EMPTY SPACES

I've noticed in my own life and in those of my students, friends, and colleagues that the lightening of our loads can actually be scary. The layers of unaddressed stuff that stand between us and our goals may be uncomfortable, but they are also familiar. And it is not easy to release a familiar paradigm when we don't know what will replace it. Earlier I mentioned updating my wardrobe, and though that was fun for me, it might not be everyone's idea of a good time. And if you've let go of a primary relationship, or a habit you've come to depend on for comfort, these transitions can be nuanced and challenging.

Our opportunity is to fill those empty spaces with intention, clarity, and a fierce commitment to what we call in next. I often refer to the quote at the beginning of this chapter when I feel lost or scared about a space I have cleared. I imagine my true direction rising up from my unseen life, dreaming me into unprecedented possibilities.

BE FIERCE

What have you let go (or do you intend to let go) that makes your writing life more possible, productive, or prolific? Come to fierceonthepage.com/letitgo to share how it felt and what it's meant to your work.

DON'T SMOKE A CIGARETTE WHILE PUSHING AN OXYGEN TANK

A HABIT CANNOT BE TOSSED OUT THE WINDOW; IT MUST BE COAXED DOWN THE STAIRS A STEP AT A TIME. —*Mark Twain*

It was lunch hour downtown. I was weaving through clusters of window-shopping pedestrians, walking as fast as I could to the post office, when I saw her and stopped in my tracks.

A woman in a wheelchair was using her feet to shuffle herself forward. An oxygen tank was rigged up behind her right shoulder, sending life support through twin plastic tubes that fed into her nostrils. And dangling from her mouth was a lit cigarette.

The sight of this woman filled me with compassion for the human experience. It struck me that we all have some version of this woman inside of us. As we negotiate the medicines and poisons of our choices, our desires, and our habits, we send out mixed messages about what we want and need.

The fact is, most of us are so accustomed to creating interference that limits our performance and stunts our results that we have grown blind to the absurdities of our contradictions. We shuffle along until that moment of truth, when someone stops in their tracks, looks at us, and gasps.

Let's take a look at how we can avoid gawkers in the street, shall we?

SEEK OUT INTERFERENCE

You can anticipate and intercept the areas in your life where you are misaligned by recognizing how your behaviors do not express your goals and values. This can help inform new choices about the way you write (and live). Do you recognize yourself in any of these questions?

- Do you have difficulty prioritizing writing time?
- Do you fear completing a project because it might not be perfect enough?
- Do you have a desire to publish your work but don't send it out?
- Do you have some other goal that you haven't found a way to fulfill?
- Do you miss deadlines and opportunities?
- Do you fail to follow through on your promises to yourself or your writing community?
- Are you unclear about your priorities?
- Do your failures, mistakes, and disappointments stop you from trying again?

If your intention and behavior are out of sync, I believe you need something more powerful, more effective, and more fundamentally aligned with human nature than discipline to return you to alignment.

PUT DOWN THAT CIGARETTE

I believe the job of all writers is to elevate the desire to write (or publish, or meet a deadline, or break through fear) so far above the desire for the cigarette (or lesser habit) that it becomes the inevitable choice to pick up the pen instead of the lighter each time you're looking for a fix.

If you're not meeting your goals, chances are good that your idea of what you want hasn't yet been ignited by or aligned with your true desire. And when you're not making choices from that vital urgency of desire, you can be quite easily distracted.

Let's resuscitate your relationship with oxygen and tackle that cigarette habit.

In my experience, it's far easier to add a good habit than to break a bad one. Add enough good habits and you simply crowd out the behaviors you don't want. They become less interesting and less compelling. For example, when I wanted to elevate my physical well-being, I started by adding two enormous servings of vegetables to my daily diet. Then, because I love to dance, I added Zumba twice a week. Next, I added three weekly runs on the treadmill (which I didn't enjoy much at first) while watching every episode of every season of *The West Wing* (which I enjoyed a great deal).

The more I added, the better I felt. The more I paired activities I didn't particularly cherish with ones I eagerly anticipated, the more momentum I gained. The better I felt, the less inclined I was to make choices that didn't feel good. With my new vitality boost, I started noticing which foods added to my energy supply, and I ate more of those. I then had less room for those foods that drained me. Over time, it stopped occurring to me to eat foods that were not adding real nutritional value. In the end, instead of having an epic power struggle to cut sugar from my diet, I reduced its hold on me by filling up on more sustainable sweetness in life. And I became hooked on feeling vital.

Let's consider how this approach can translate to your writing life. I'm going to propose for the sake of example that you want to make writing a bigger slice of your pie. What can you add to make it happen? Consider some of these possibilities.

- **ADD ACCOUNTABILITY.** You could add a daily e-mail check-in about your writing progress with a writing buddy, a coach, your mother, a colleague—someone who cares about whether you meet your goals and is excited to cheer you on. You could schedule a reading of your current work-in-progress for some time in the future so that you must finish by that date. Or you can promise your blog readers that you'll post at certain intervals (they'll know if you don't) or finish a larger project by a certain time—and then report on it.
- **ADD MOTIVATION.** Why are you called to write more? Will it help you pay the bills? Bolster your entomologist platform so you get more speaking gigs about arachnids? Will it make you look cool in front of

the girls? How can you infuse yourself with this motivation to keep you coming back for more?

- **ADD FUN**. What makes writing more fun? If you don't know, experiment. Drinking tea and sitting at the keyboard with a cat in my lap makes writing more fun for me. Could you get your feet massaged while writing, or sit in a mountain chalet, in front of a fire? Could you listen to disco or ocean sounds to establish the mood from which you want to create? Could you take a dance break every fifteen minutes?

- **ADD FOCUS**. What gets your attention focused on writing? Taking a notebook with you to the woods? Turning off your Internet connection? Burying the phone in the backyard? Closing the door to the room where you're working? Setting a timer to keep you on task? Many writers shut down social media to improve their focus, but some say keeping it going actually provides a kind of background noise that gets them in the zone. Your job is to experiment with input and context to see what works for you.

- **ADD COMMUNITY**. Could other people encourage you to write more? Experiment with a daily, weekly, or monthly writing date with a friend or a writing group. Join a critique group where you can regularly share feedback, publishing ideas, craft insights, and snacks. Sit in a café to write, and steep in the human hubbub of conversation and stimulus. Invite your family to handle dinner prep and cleanup so you can get two extra hours for writing, or ask them to honor your office hours or to support your weekend writing retreat.

- **ADD URGENCY**. Set an aggressive deadline—and meet it. Or set microdeadlines—such as posting a small amount of your writing online at regular intervals. (I once blogged every day for a year to challenge myself to produce more content. It's how I convinced myself I could write a book.)

- **ADD COMPASSION**. As you transition to the state of wanting oxygen more than wanting cigarettes, you'll experience setbacks. You'll get lost and confused and unsure. You'll revert. It's okay; we all do. You might think you don't deserve the oxygen, or you might still be inhaling the last drag of Mr. Sharkman's unflattering words about you in fourth grade. This is your time to let go and detox from all of those old stories and beliefs as you fill up on new thoughts and viewpoints that serve you better. When you find yourself wandering away from where you want to be, ask yourself what you can add to call yourself back. Then add some—and then some more. And you'll be on your way back to center.

I think Mark Twain was almost right. When you throw a habit out the window, it just comes running right back up the stairs for you. But when you invest yourself in new and better habits, the ones you'd like to part with eventually find their own way down the stairs and out into the great, fertile compost of your past, through which your desired future regenerates.

TAKE A STAND

It has taken me more than twenty years of writing seriously to understand what is, for this writer, far more essential than having a platform, knowing my audience, or targeting particular publications. At the root of all this strategic-marketing stuff, which is of great importance but should come a little later, is knowing where I stand as a writer and as a person.

What does this mean, and how does a writer get to the point of knowing?

Over the years, my writing was a kite on the winds of influence, opinion, and inner disorientation. First, I wrote to survive. Later, I wrote to give service and make connections. Though I'd defined all of the strategic stuff mentioned above (and I love the strategic stuff), I remained a somewhat shapeless self, roaming around within my many PowerPoint presentations of carefully articulated goals. This writer-self, I now realize, was still seeking the right landing pad, one that she would never reach via goals and platforms. She simply hadn't found a means to achieving what she desired.

It was only through my divorce journey, and as I started writing content for my Radical Divorce blog and class, that I came to my latest layer of understanding about what it means to find one's authority as a person and as a writer. I made a choice about how I intended to move through my divorce. My guiding principles were emotional honesty, self-responsibility, and optimism. I made a decision that the writing I did would be processed through these filters as well, with emotional truths winning out over optimism when the two were profoundly in conflict. In so doing, I understood for the first time that this was more than a short-term survival strategy or a writing maneuver: These were the guiding principles of my life.

With this realization, my focus became absolute. Now I was writing to first define and then learn how to occupy an identity and a context that had significance for me. It was almost as if I were a cartoon person waiting for my house and garden to be drawn around me. Through this lens, everything that I'd done and written in my life had new meaning and relevance.

Whatever my platform might be or the publications that line its shelves, I know I can count on myself to show up on the page in a way that respects my own pain and that of others, focuses on the opportunities and gifts that such agonies bring, and offers love for the ever-floundering, ever-flawed, ever-extraordinary human condition.

It's almost as if I've stumbled upon the secret fountain of my soul that's been the water source of my life all this time but was unnamed and therefore unreachable. Today, I name this soul fountain "Grace." I take a stand for grace. I live and write to occupy the space where all that happens is welcome, all who enter are welcome, and all that is available to me is not only within reach but deeply appreciated.

BE FIERCE

What do you take a stand for in your life and in your writing, and how does it change everything to consciously acknowledge it? I'd love to hear what you are discovering at fierceonthepage.com/takeastand.

FAIL HARDER

BY WRITING POETRY, EVEN THOSE POEMS THAT FAIL AND FAIL MISERABLY, WE HONOR AND AFFIRM LIFE. WE SAY, WE LOVED THE EARTH BUT COULD NOT STAY. —*Ted Kooser*

The reader had given me a five-star review of my book. She spent a few paragraphs raving about all she had learned, and then she dedicated the entire second half of the review to venting about a typo that displeased her. Reading this review brought me back to my own long and circuitous journey living alongside the inevitability of mistakes.

Like this miffed reviewer, I was once the kind of writer who would not have forgiven myself for that typo. For any typo. When I was that kind of writer—an imaginary perfect writer—I did not send my work out for fear that it contained a flaw. In fact, I did not share it with anyone, ever. What if my writing was no good? What if other people didn't like it? What if, heaven forbid, the writing contained a mistake?

I remember the day when I made a decision that changed my writing life forever. I was attending an event at the ad agency Wieden+Kennedy and stumbled upon an enormous pushpin mural that said, simply, "Fail Harder."

What an invitation! I felt like I had stumbled upon my own proverbial wizard behind the curtain. That poor, beaten-down wizard, whose failures had been completely misunderstood and unappreciated. I felt, for a moment, a kind of failure pride. I took a deep breath into the revelation that failing hard is often in direct proportion to trying hard—something I valued greatly. And I considered: What if failing harder could actually be the path that led me where I wanted to go? What if imperfection was my jet fuel? What if I could have both the five-star review *and* the typo?

In Japan, *wabi-sabi* is an aesthetic rooted in the art of imperfection, a celebration of the flaw that makes a piece of art (or a life) unique. When you embrace imperfection in your writing, you welcome the human condition as the source of your writing. This helps you cultivate the compassion and acceptance that you (and your writing) deserve. And it helps you learn to trust your deep reservoirs of material and insight instead of punishing yourself and strangling your creative process for fear of making a mistake.

When you set your sights on perfection, it's easy to forget that mistakes yield some of the richest and most surprising material—insights, wisdom, and writing that is not accessible through so-called success. James Joyce proclaimed mistakes to be the portal to discovery. In my experience, mistakes often turn out to be such enormous gifts that I eventually don't even consider the initial disappointment or embarrassment a mistake. What you detest and want most to avoid or hide—the fumbles and the foibles and those horribly embarrassing, awkward moments— make you vulnerable enough to connect with other humans. And with your own higher guidance. Who could penetrate a slick wall of perfection? And who would want to?

I used to believe that when I stood in front of people to speak or read, I had to pretend to be someone other then myself in order to impress my audience. Because I am a terrible actor, pretending to be someone impressive made me stiff, awkward, and awful. Eventually, I decided that good enough was good enough. That perfection was not the point. That sharing writing that mattered to me and making an authentic connection was far more important. And if people judged me for my imperfect work, so be it.

When I wore a wrap that kept falling off my shoulder and onto the page I was trying to read from, when I cried uncontrollably while reading the scar poem I had written, when I confessed to getting it all wrong and then rearranged my outfit, got a tissue, and started reading again, my audience was with me. They were included in my struggle to navigate vulnerability alongside strength while making an authentic offering.

What I thought would alienate me from others actually created a greater intimacy among us. And the mistakes I made taught me over time what it takes to make a meaningful presentation: how to stay on topic and on schedule, how to choose clothing that would stay on, how to present the right mix of content and connection, and how to adapt on the fly to audience interest and disinterest. Such that I have come to consider a flaw as not merely something we learn to tolerate, but as a distinguishing mark that honors the great effort we have made in our work, just as laugh lines underscore a life well lived.

The Japanese art of Kintsugi involves mending broken objects by filling the cracks with gold—to illuminate the repair and honor an object's history of usefulness rather than to try to disguise the damage. If the typo that runs through my book is a fissure, my attitude about that mistake can be the vein of gold. I tell myself, "I wrote a book! Yes, there were mistakes. Mistakes happen when humans make things. Not everyone will approve of my offering. Some will focus on the flaws. It's okay. This is the physics of vulnerability. You will keep trying hard, failing hard, and learning as you go."

It's also important to keep in mind that what you consider "failure" can shape-shift before your eyes as your contexts and interpretations change. A friend was recently talking about all the years and all the money she spent in graduate school becoming an expert in a field she quickly realized she had no desire to practice in. She eventually concluded that paying off loans for years to come was completely worth it—because she met her lovely husband in grad school.

This is how life goes. We expend tremendous resources in what proves to be the "wrong direction." And yet there are equally tremendous—and often unexpected—riches to be sourced from every "mistake." In fact, the mistakes are far more valuable than the successes. You went to grad school to establish your career, and instead you established your family. You were devastated not to publish those five novels, but as they composted into dream material in a box under your bed, the themes reshuffled and cohered into the taproot of a fresh, new story.

When you don't get what you wanted, or when someone hurts you, or when you disappoint yourself to the brink of devastation, this is not the end of the story. Sooner or later, the pain you feel becomes a kind of transportation, and you arrive somewhere else that never could have been accessible without that vehicle. Often, you end up somewhere even better than where you originally set your heart on going. And in this new place, you are anchored by wisdom. Seasoned by trust. Humbled and grateful for all you didn't get—all you once you thought you wanted.

I invite you to write your own bylaws about the paradoxes of authenticity and perfection, failure and success. Consider the ways in which you straightjacket your creativity with some ideal of how you are supposed to be. And when you look back on those mistakes that make you cringe, look a little closer to see if new growth is unfurling through the fissures. See if you can find your gold.

BE FIERCE

Have you made a doozy of a mistake lately? If so, I applaud you! Let's celebrate it together at fierceonthepage.com/failharder. If you haven't, I dare you to put more skin in the game. Without mistakes, you're missing some very important vistas. Every misstep gives you a foothold into growth, compassion, and greater clarity about what you want and how to get there. Getting it wrong is the foundation on which getting it right is built. I dare you to fail harder. And then go out and fail some more, while living (and writing) the life you always wanted.

THE ART OF INCUBATION

WE DO NOT KNOW UNTIL THE SHELL BREAKS WHAT KIND OF EGG WE HAVE BEEN SITTING ON. —*T.S. Eliot*

When we are not actively working toward a stated goal, we tend to call it procrastination. Often this is accurate. However, procrastination is sometimes confused with *incubation*, the process of ruminating and allowing ideas the time they need to take root.

Nobody looks at a six-months-pregnant woman and says, "Oh, she's procrastinating. If she were a real achiever, she would have given birth to that baby already." Nor do we expect that when we plant cucumber seeds in the garden soil that we'll be harvesting cucumbers the following week. We all understand that birth and plant growth have their own time lines independent of our ideas and agendas.

Without incubation time, the natural cycles of life would not exist. So it is with writing. The challenge is that the writing life doesn't have finite gestation periods defined by the seasons of planting and harvest. Each of us must determine for ourselves when it's time to move from idea to incubation, and then to action.

I had the first reflection of my own incubation process at my first communications job at age twenty-five, where I was writing educational materials for behavioral health plan members. One day a team member who managed the database for our vast inventory of materials reported me to my boss when she noticed me looking out the window, "doing nothing." In fact, I was struggling to come up with a way to say something meaningful to parents of teenage kids about navigating transition. But this inner inquiry was of course not visible to my colleague.

This is why incubation is tricky—it doesn't look like much. A bird sits on an egg, a seed whispers its secrets beneath our hearing, a woman stares out the window.

Henri Poincaré, a legendary French mathematician and philosopher of science and polymath, proposed that creativity happens in four steps.

1. **PREPARATION**: We set our intentions and define our goals.
2. **INCUBATION**: We dream into the possibilities, honor the unknown, and become receptive to what is seeking us.
3. **ILLUMINATION**: We have the revelation in which some new possibility takes shape.
4. **EXECUTION**: We create to manifest and materialize our discovery.

In the rush to cross the finish line, I see many writers leap straight to execution without having first grappled with what they are striving for, then entered the requisite realm of complete disorientation that the road to illumination seems to require of us.

Execution without vision is like a house without a foundation. When you incubate, you are waiting for the cement of your intent to dry before building the edifice.

What does incubation look like exactly, and how long does it take? This differs for each writer, and even for each project that writer undertakes. In chapter seventy, I share a story about a time when I simply could not force myself from incubation to illumination, despite my ambition. Some pieces of writing take a lifetime to complete, while others are written in a weekend. Your job as a writer is not to set a clock to tell you how to move through the stages of creativity, but to listen to and honor your own process. Dragging your heels or moving too fast can confuse your literary circadian rhythms and make it difficult to do your best work.

I believe that procrastination—which is born from fear—often happens between steps three and four of Poincaré's process, in a kind of limbo between illumination and execution. Though you may recognize the direction your work is taking, you have a crisis of confidence that prevents you from taking the next necessary steps. This is a very different phenomenon from incubation, in which you have a goal or a vision and steep in the mysteries until a new possibility for creation coheres within.

The more closely you pay attention to your own process, the more easily you can identify what's moving you ahead and what's holding you back in your writing life. When you are willing to sit on the egg as long as necessary, then take action when the shell breaks, you are allowing the art of incubation to serve your writing.

BE FIERCE

How do you distinguish between incubation and procrastination in your writing life? Are you giving yourself enough space to become receptive to illumination? How can you build in some breathing room and hold space for what you are inviting in? When could slowing down actually be the most efficient way to move toward your goal? Share what you're discovering with us at fierceonthepage.com/artofincubation. Let's see if we can go deeper into our understanding and practice of incubation.

SECURE YOUR OWN MASK BEFORE ASSISTING OTHERS

If you've traveled by airplane, you've experienced the attendant who instructs passengers before takeoff to secure their own oxygen mask before assisting others in the event of an in-flight emergency. I believe our writing lives could benefit from the same advisory warning.

Secure your own mask before assisting others. If I had to name a single principle for helper types like myself to live and work by, it would be this.

So many of us writers work at least two full-time jobs (one as a writer and another that either provides our primary income source or provides primary care for our family—or both) and make constant compromises and sacrifices to keep ourselves, our passion, our families, and our sanity intact.

We are no good to others if we are not good to ourselves first. This much I know. So how do we live by this principle?

I propose that we start by defining our own terms.

What does it mean to you to secure your own mask before assisting others? What are the essentials you must have in place to provide the foundation of energy you need to make your writing life happen—and to create the overflow resources you need to give to all the people and causes you wish to serve?

Here is my "secure your own mask" list, in priority order:

1. **SLEEP**: I get at least eight hours a night, if at all possible.
2. **FINANCIAL SECURITY**: The mortgage and bills are comfortably covered.

3. **QUALITY TIME WITH MY FAMILY**: I know specifically what this means to me in terms of the types of activities, the amount of time, and the shared feeling of the experience.

4. **WORK COMMITMENTS FULFILLED**: Deadlines are met, my desk is cleared, and I have a clear vision for the next day, week, and project.

5. **WRITING VISION ARTICULATED, IF NOT ENACTED**: I know what I intend to do so that I can hit the ground running (and writing) when a window of time appears in which to write.

6. **SELF-CARE PRACTICE**: I walk the dog every morning and take a bath before bed every night, no matter what.

7. **FUN**: Because I have a tendency to fill every spare moment with work, I make guidelines for when and how I intend to have fun. Then I stick to them.

When I'm in balance, my client work gets done, my family and I have a blast, and my creative endeavors have the space they need to breathe and meet me at the page. I'll bet you find the same to be true.

When you establish a steady flow of oxygen for your life and your writing, you'll be better prepared to follow through on your commitments to yourself and to others. The writing you produce and the experience of those around you will likely improve, too.

It's okay if you don't know exactly what you need yet. All you need to do is commit to finding out.

BE FIERCE

Try making a "secure your own mask" list based on what you know works and doesn't work for you today. Then experiment with the variables that are foundational to your well-being. Make note of what energizes and what drains you. For instance, you could discover that your exercise regimen is time-consuming but actually doubles your energy (and therefore gives you extra time for your writing). Or you may be surprised by the source of an energy leak, which you could plug with a clear boundary, such as talking on the phone to your distressed friend for a half hour instead of two hours. The better you know and honor what you need, the better equipped you will be to give service to your family, readers, clients, customers, colleagues, and everyone (and everything) else that matters most to you.

LEARN THE NAMES OF THINGS

On the cusp of age three-and-a-half, my son, Theo, was going through a growth spurt. Suddenly breakfast became a two-hour-long affair (made possible by his 5 A.M. waking time) where I paraded out every food imaginable and he ate it all.

One morning, as he was making his way through a mosaic of plates holding eggs, nuts, fruit, cheese, yogurt, and cereal, we stumbled upon a new ritual: catalog surfing. And not the type you'd expect.

A bed and bath catalog sat on the counter, waiting to be recycled. Without thinking, I opened it. Theo was captivated. He'd never seen such a thing.

"Read it to me?" he suggested.

"It's mostly a list of colors," I explained.

"I want to hear the colors!" was his emphatic response.

My son is articulate. The spirit driving his articulation, even in his earliest years, has been the pleasure of naming his visual, physical, and emotional experiences. Earlier that morning he observed, for example, how his lozenge resembled a sea anemone and then described what happens when the lozenge "dissipated." Of course he would want to experience the sensory promises of a catalog. Suddenly it seemed silly that this had never occurred to me before.

I turned a glossy page and began: *amethyst, ivory, lemon chiffon, linen, mint, sky, taupe, toast, pool, eggshell, fennel, marzipan, rose water, sandalwood, sea glass.* The list went on and on and on. I had never spoken a catalog's worth of color before. Theo and I were swimming in a sea of sensory suggestion.

As I moved toward the back half of the catalog, no longer able to take in the meaning of the words I was speaking, I recalled a poetry reading in graduate school featuring my professor, the great poet Galway Kinnell.

At the end of the reading, a young man asked Galway, "If you could give one piece of advice to poets, what would it be?"

Galway said, "Learn the names of things."

This is the impulse behind all writing: the desire to liberate knowledge, insight, emotion, and truth. When we learn the vocabulary of any topic—insects, dinosaurs, solar systems, or bath towels, for example—we transcend time, space, and form, and we get to experience particular realms through the specificity of language. The names of things are the keys that unlock such raptures. Language is the secret knock standing between us and limitless, virtual (and actual) experience. It's such a small but potent act to hold the name of a thing inside you—and then to share it.

As Theo sat rapt, taking in my staccato of sensory description, we initiated ourselves into the vocabulary and promise of bed-and-bath comfort. I was reminded that when a speaker (or writer) and a listener (or reader) are paired, the circuit is complete, and the possibilities of how words can alchemize us are endless.

BE FIERCE

What vocabulary could you dive into to make a piece of writing more vivid? Does one of your characters have a vocation or avocation that invites you and your readers into a new realm of sound and suggestion? How could you electrify your sense of what is possible in language by studying a field guide for birds or a manual for building an engine or the biography of a muralist? How does learning the names of things open the aperture to what you see?

EMBRACE YOUR ENVY

Rick Springfield came on stage with guitars blazing. When the aging rocker moaned, "Jessie's got himself a girl, and I want to make her mine ..." the crowd went berserk. We were an audience of all ages, races, and backgrounds, swept up in a wave of passion, belting out in unison, "I wish that I had Jessie's girl!"

For me, this sing-along conjured the sweetest of preteen angst. Clearly, I was not alone. For more than three decades, "Jessie's Girl" has been striking a chord that runs through us all. Wanting what someone else has is a universal human experience. For Rick Springfield, envy is the secret sauce behind the hit single that defined his career. For the rest of us, envy can be equally potent in accelerating our ability to realize our ambitions and fulfill our dreams.

Think of how your leg feels if you've been sitting on it for too long and it's gone to sleep. The waking-up process feels like pins and needles prickling beneath your skin, and probably involves some awkward hopping around before full comfort and balance are restored. Envy can be like this.

When you find yourself envying another writer's accomplishment, it awakens your own desires—or stokes them. This can feel pretty uncomfortable, especially if you've repressed your desire out of fear or discouragement.

Everything depends on what you choose to make of this uncomfortable moment.

When you tell yourself, "He got it, so I can't have it," as if only one publishing deal, speaking opportunity, or literary honor existed, you create a roadblock of story between you and your awakened desire. The leg goes back to sleep. It's comfortable enough in its mute numbness—though of course you can't walk.

When you say instead, "There is enough of what he has to go around, and I intend to be the next person to get it," and then stomp that foot a few times and breathe through the pins and needles, you'll be up on your feet again in no time and can start manifesting what you desire.

"But I want Jesse's girl, and there's only one of those," insists your inner Rick Springfield. Right?

Let's investigate this premise. What exactly does Jesse's girl have that Rick wants—and how can he go about getting it? If it is a particular quality he appreciates, it can likely be found in other, available girls. Or maybe what Rick really wants is to be more like Jesse. In which case he can consider refining the behaviors or habits or hairstyle that he admires in his friend.

Through this exploration, he may discover that he's not actually suited for Jesse's girl but instead clarifies that he's just ready for a relationship—with someone else. Or maybe he realizes that he was merely competing with Jesse—and that his envy had nothing to do with the girl.

For writers, envy can manifest in endless ways. Maybe someone in your writing group is awarded a writing residency, and you discover that you yearn for a stretch of uninterrupted writing time. Now you have an opportunity to explore how to make it possible. Or maybe a poet you have been following on social media seems to get published in all the journals you admire and have not yet been published in. You can study how that poet's work is well suited for those publications and use that insight to find journals that are likely seeking poems like yours. For example, let's say he writes language poetry and you write lyric poetry; his ability to place his poems where they are celebrated can inform your own search for publications that will appreciate yours. Or maybe you attend a lecture on craft, and you're annoyed that the speaker doesn't seem to be any better informed than you are. Through your irritation, you discover that you have a desire to share what you know with others. So you start investigating local forums for teaching and speaking about the topics in which you are an expert.

See? This isn't about taking Jesse's girl. It's about identifying the spark of desire that Jesse and his girl ignite in you, and then delighting in the quest this sends you on to discover who you are called to be (and be with).

We're conditioned to think envy is bad, because we think there isn't enough of the type of success we want to go around. But when we consider envy to be a point of desire, and we believe that one person's good news does not preclude our own, we can enjoy discovering fresh desire and get curious about the best way to fulfill it.

Let's remember that when we see other people doing or getting some version of what we want, *we have proof that it is possible*!

When envy comes up in your writing life, I propose that you don't subdue it in the name of propriety and good citizenry. I hope you do the opposite: Investigate it until you get to that place in you that says, *I want, I need, I DESIRE*. Stay with the tears as long as you need to, and walk off those pins and needles. Then buckle your seatbelt and get your pens and keyboards ready, because life takes such clarity seriously.

CULTIVATE YOUR VOICE

ATTENTION FOR YOUR WORK IS NOT A BIRTHRIGHT. TO STAND OUT, YOU MUST DEVELOP AN AUTHENTIC, COMPELLING VOICE.
—Todd Henry

A student asked me recently how I attracted an audience when I started blogging in 2006. I explained to her that my entire purpose at that time was to write well, write daily, and keep going. I wasn't thinking about an audience, and I wasn't hoping for one. I was striving to publish something online every day as if I had readers counting on me to do so. This discipline was an experiment to see if I could stay accountable to a daily writing practice, one in which I pressed myself to do quality work quickly and then "go live" at the end of the writing session.

Somehow people started finding my work, commenting on it, and sharing it. And pretty soon, I had a little community of bloggers around the globe whom I adored. Reading and responding to each other's blogs every day was our version of gathering around the virtual water cooler. A little tribe of thinkers, writers, and adorers was born.

Over time, I learned through this community that what I was doing wasn't as purely "literary" as I had originally thought. Through the conversations I had and the readers I attracted, I came to understand that what I was writing had spiritual resonance. Everything I wanted to know and wanted to write was tinged with an ache to inhabit my humanity more fully, more comprehensibly. I was writing as a means of teaching myself how to live. Through the eyes and the feedback of my writing community, I came to understand that this personal quest was what distinguished my literary voice.

I wasn't able to answer my student's question satisfactorily because I don't know exactly how my first blog and I entered the orbit of this lovely literary tribe. But I do know that it was a natural evolution that grew from people wanting to read my writing. With that traction and encouragement, eventually I launched new blogs focused on serving specific audiences. And for these later projects, I developed and implemented a strategy for attracting and sustaining the interest of readers.

What worked for me, and what I believe works for all writers, is to first give our absolute devotion to what we have to say and how we say it. This is what makes us magnetic to readers. Process and practice are vital—but only when they are a means to elevating your craft. Readers are not going to seek out your work because you have a great social media strategy, or because you kept your butt in the chair to write from 6 to 7 A.M. every day this week, or because you found a way to meet the submission deadline. These practices are the means to an end: discovering, developing, and sharing your unique voice. Readers will give you their attention when you offer them an original, memorable voice that affects them deeply.

When U.S. Supreme Court Justice Potter Stewart was asked to define obscenity in 1964, the best he could do was to say, "I know it when I see it." Voice is also an elusive concept, but I think we all know it when we see it—which is why I advise studying the writers you admire. You might also consider how Stanley Kunitz, Sylvia Plath, Charles Bukowski, and Jane Kenyon each navigate grief. If you are familiar with these poets' work, chances are good that you'd be able to match poet to poem effortlessly. Think of the writers and poets on your bookshelves. What do you turn to them for, and why? How does it feel to imbibe their words?

I consider voice the intermingling of spirit, intention, and language that makes a poet or writer's work distinctly his own.

Our job as writers is to infuse our work with the passion of our purpose. To inform *what* we are writing with *why* we are writing it. When you know what you stand for and the impact you want to have, this comes through in your writing.

No matter how thoughtfully architected your writing may be, I believe that what you share in stories, essays, screenplays, articles, and poems is not inherently compelling. Mary Oliver advises, "Attention without feeling is only a report." It's how you deliver your work, the voice through which it enters the reader's nervous system, that makes all the difference. Even in business writing, when the writer must adapt himself to an objective that is not personal, the raw material of his voice always shines through.

So before you jump on the "get published fast" bandwagon and start experimenting with strategies to sell your manuscript, gain visibility, or grow an audience, I suggest that you invest first in developing a voice that you feel proud to share. This is the most reliable starting place toward putting your work in the hands of more readers.

Your readers (or the readers you will eventually attract) want to hear the work the way *you* tell it. They want your words in their ear, your characters, images, and intonations flashing across their screen. They choose you to give them the struggle, the loss, the resolution, the remedy, the glimpse into the human experience.

Your voice is the reader's portal to your work. The more you dedicate yourself to refining it, the more likely readers will seek you out for it.

GET BACK ON THE SCALE

When my bathroom scale stopped working shortly after my son, Theo, was born, I shoved it under the couch. Three years later, I pulled it out, replaced the battery, and—voilà—the scale blinked its big, bright, digital eyes at me once again.

No big deal, right? One would think.

Except that, for three years, this simple task seemed insurmountable. The central processing system of my mind was completely overloaded with all that I was responsible for: supporting a family, mothering an infant, promoting a book, writing and then promoting another. And because I had no resources to devote to solving this small problem, I had accepted the scale's defunct status as final. The secondary benefit, of course, was that I did not have to weigh myself.

I wasn't sleeping, I wasn't exercising—heck, I barely had time to shower—and I was riding on the fumes of simple carbs and chai tea lattes to get through each day physically and emotionally. If I didn't know what I weighed, some voice in me argued, I was somehow off the hook of reclaiming the lightness and vitality that had previously been my norm.

During those years without the scale, I thought I was saving myself from the pain of the facts. But as it turns out, the pain inflicted by my imagination was far worse. When I got on the scale once again, I was surprised to find that I weighed much less than I had imagined. I was shaped differently, without a doubt, but I was back to my pre-pregnancy weight and probably had been for years. Just by getting on the scale, I shed the mental weight I'd been carrying. And I was finally ready to invite a vibrant life force to return to my body.

What does this have to do with you and your writing life? Everything. Because I'll bet you the chai tea latte I skipped this morning that you are avoiding something in your writing life with as much dedication and justification as I was avoiding my scale. You can't manage what you don't measure, as the old adage goes. And by putting your head in the sand, you are depriving yourself of opportunities to meet your writing life head-on. Sure, it's uncomfortable to review your submission binder and note that you haven't sent out work for eight months, ever since you were flatlined by your last rejection. It may be no fun to dig out that unfinished piece you hid in the back of your file cabinet after the thirteenth round of edits and to look at it with fresh eyes.

But the truth is also the very best medicine. Facing every dusty corner of your broken promises and sloppy habits is your best hope for creating the writing life you want. In fact, chances are good that as it simmered in your file cabinet, the plot knot in your abandoned story may have simply untangled itself and now you know how to resolve it. And your submission binder might feel inviting after a long hiatus. At worst, you'll have a bit more perspective and emotional distance to perceive what you need to do next to move toward what you want most.

It's never too late to get back on the scale, measure how you're living up to your goals for your writing life, and then take informed action. Buddha reportedly said, "What you are is what you have been. What you'll be is what you do now."

Let's say your goal is to submit a personal essay to a writing contest in six weeks, and you plan to write from 6 to 7 A.M. every weekday until then to meet that goal. If you're recording your progress in your calendar or on your office whiteboard every day, you can easily see over time if your practice is lining up with your intention. When you bring daily attention to your choices, you can quickly course-correct.

For example, if you notice you skipped two days of writing, you can consider what the holdup is. Let's say you find that starting at 6 A.M. is hard to do, because you have to get your family out the door to school and work at 7:30 A.M. Perhaps you can experiment with writing from 5 to 6 A.M., or for an hour before bed instead.

If you get to day thirty of your commitment and you've managed only two writing sessions in the entire month, re-evaluate your goal. Maybe that contest isn't important to you after all. Or maybe it's time to recommit to your writing practice and find new strategies for making the writing time happen—such as devoting yourself to a single five-hour session each week rather than a shorter daily session.

The more you measure, the better you will understand what you're doing and if it's serving you. This insight equips you to design your writing life in the way that feels most vital and enables you to create the results you want.

BE FIERCE

Is there some part of your writing life that you have been afraid to address directly? What small step might you take right now to face that fear and move through it? You might be more ready or more capable of forging ahead than you thought. What are you doing today that's working well? How can you measure it over time, so you can find ways to do more of what serves you best?

JOIN THE CONVERSATION

In addition to producing remarkable work, writers today are also expected to grow a platform and attract an audience. If this feels pushy, inauthentic, or just plain difficult, I would like to suggest an alternative cosmology: Instead of thinking of your writing as a product you are selling, think of it as an offering you are making.

When you write, you are giving service. You are offering the very best of yourself to the world. When you change your mind-set from, "Am I good enough? Will anybody want what I'm offering?" to "How can I help?" your inner conversation shifts from one centered around ego to one that is far more resourced and sure.

We all have something to give that matters deeply to us—and to others. When this spirit of generosity is your compass, the way you engage with others is transformed.

Over the years, I found that my passion for helping writers find their way forward overrode my own insecurities about whether I had anything meaningful to share. I wanted people to read what I wrote, not because I wanted to sell them more stuff but because I hoped beyond hope that it would invite them to experience greater freedom and joy with their writing process and results. Let's consider how you might offer something similar to your readers.

MAKE A CONTRIBUTION

What do you hope beyond hope to contribute? And how can you embody that generosity of spirit with every conversation you have? Whether you are attending a reading, meeting with your writing group, visiting a bookstore, or conversing online, I propose that you simply strive to enter the conversation. When you authentically share, listen, and respond to your writing community, you powerfully enrich your own life and the lives of your readers (or potential readers).

PRODUCE, CONSUME, AND SHARE MEANINGFUL CONTENT

An important part of making an authentic connection is producing meaningful content. In today's connected world, content is currency. This is very good news for writers. When you have meaningful things to say, share, synthesize, and celebrate, you are more likely to stay connected with people who share your interests. By content, I mean the stuff you read, write, collect, and share on blogs, social media, and print and online news and entertainment sources, such as how-to tips, genre-specific information, observations about the literary landscape, craft insights and instruction, interviews, advice, inspiration, book reviews, poems, and quotes.

The more you engage with the content you collect and generate, and the more you participate in the content your community offers, the better you can get to know yourself and what you have to offer in the context of the larger conversation of your life and your tribe. You can learn the needs of the people you serve or wish to serve. You can let the successes of other writers inspire and motivate you. And you can engage with people who share your values and passions.

Consuming content is the path to generating content. Generating content can be a meaningful path toward understanding who you are as a writer, what you are called to offer, and who is attracted to reading it. Every conversation you have is a seed of connection that could eventually blossom into friendship, collaboration, or an opportunity to contribute.

SEEK THE CONNECTIONS THAT BUILD COMMUNITY

Not sure who your literary tribe is yet? Start sharing what matters to you, and they'll find you. Start reading what matters to you, and you'll find them. You can also join meetups or online communities organized around a topic that interests you, search hashtags for keywords that are relevant to you, ask Google who's trending in your field, and attend workshops, readings, and lectures.

CROSS-FERTILIZE

Cross-fertilization is a powerful way to contribute through content. When you showcase another person's work (by sharing a post or link or featuring a colleague in an interview, for example) it helps her become more visible with your readers, and it can bring her readers to you. When you offer content to another person (such as by writing a guest post or being interviewed on his podcast), it can help him build credibility with his readers and help you connect with his audience, while providing something they want or need.

BE CONTEXT SPECIFIC

Keep in mind that most of us have multiple contexts in which we write, live, and serve. That's why it is important to be aware of and intentional about your role in each conversation you have. When I post in the community forum for entrepreneurs building digital businesses, for example, I don't share my thoughts about the craft of poetry. And when I'm writing a post on my blog for writers, I'm not likely to discuss the relative merits of lead generation software. As I discussed in greater detail in chapter twelve, you build credibility and real connection with your audiences by having the conversations they come to you to have.

BE FIERCE

When you consider the conversations you have and the content you produce as field research for understanding your literary landscape, you are most likely to discover who you are, what you have to offer, who might be interested in your offerings, the questions and needs of your audience, and the composition of the community you want to learn with or from.

Join the conversation, and make a meaningful contribution. This is how I believe an audience is authentically attracted and a platform is sustainably built.

CLAIM YOUR SUPERPOWER;
CHERISH YOUR KRYPTONITE

I am not a natural driver. The literal skill and focus required to operate a motor vehicle does not come easily to my figurative mind. When I first got my permit and set out to practice with my father in the passenger's seat, I drove us directly into a busy, four-way intersection. I'd missed the stop sign and the oncoming traffic because I was acutely aware that a boy who had recently dumped me without explanation lived in the development to my left. This distraction had created an overwhelming magnetic pull through which I could "see" nothing actual in that moment beyond my own teenage ache.

Unfortunately, the distraction of boys wasn't the only problem with my capacity behind the wheel. Maps and road signs were completely incomprehensible to me. Plus, I had no memory of how to find the familiar places my parents had been driving me to for the past seventeen years because I'd never paid attention. During childhood car rides I had been busy doing Mad Libs, reading, trying to comprehend and sing along with Elton John or Billy Joel's harmonies, occupying seat space I refused to share with my brother, and other important tasks. It had never occurred to me to take an interest in getting from Point A to Point B, a task handled so competently by the people in charge.

Once behind the wheel, I found that the lifesaving and car-saving imperative to pay constant, single-minded attention to my surroundings and my actions was so contrary to my dream-state nature that I worked myself into a state of anxiety. Driving became a white-knuckled feat of absolute concentration that involved zero natural talent and 100 percent effort. Because tardiness made me extremely anxious and I had no idea if I'd arrive at my intended destination on the first, second, or even third attempt, I learned to build "getting lost" time into every trip.

I am a perfectionist by nature (or perhaps, in retrospect, by habit), and this disability was a source of shame and embarrassment for me. My own family had a hard time comprehending how a daughter and sister who could learn anything she set her mind to was at her developmental limit when driving.

I was so busy exerting such tremendous effort that I failed to appreciate what could only be described as a savant's knack for parallel parking. Whereas moving through interactive space eluded me, negotiating a small confine between two parked automobiles was somehow second nature. What many considered the hardest skill for a new driver to learn was my sweet spot. With a few opposing hard cuts in reverse, I could negotiate any space with inches to spare. Without thinking or trying, my body and my car knew how to do this dance intuitively.

I recently flashed back to my early driving history as I drove my brother somewhere. When we arrived at our destination, I zipped us right into the first curbside parking space I saw. My brother, the naturally skilled driver with a profoundly accurate inner GPS, was astounded. I had parallel parked with confidence and competence in a space he never would have attempted. That was when it struck me: Parallel parking was my secret superpower.

Superpowers can be quite valuable; it's handy to have a magic bullet for a specific and occasional purpose. I decided to appreciate my small and private talent for parallel parking more fully.

How does all of this relate to writing? There's a reason it took me only a few paragraphs to tell you about my secret superpower and an entire essay to describe my kryptonite. My profound driving disorientation—this inelegant, clunky, lifelong quest—has shaped me as a person and gifted me far more than ease ever could.

Being indebted to a task I am profoundly unequipped for has instilled in me a discipline of intent, a foundation of practice, and a far clearer understanding of and appreciation for my nature. I will never be a gifted driver, but I have worked hard to become an attentive and competent one. And as I struggle even today to make sense of my step-by-step Google Maps directions, I can appreciate and accept how my brain is wired. How, to me, the figurative is nectar and the literal can sometimes be a swarm of indecipherable signs.

When I was a teenager, I was ashamed that I wasn't good at everything. This clouded my ability to understand and appreciate that those Billy Joel harmonies and Mad Libs were shaping my soul. Sure, stop signs are a necessary evil, and so are cars—and I mastered those nonnative languages in time. As Theo and I decide together what songs we will shout along to as we drive, and as I scribble images, insights, and ideas on paper scraps pressed over the steering wheel at stop lights, the literal and the figurative settle in together. The superpower and the kryptonite each depend on each other for context and value.

The paradox is that my greatest vulnerability is actually the portal through which I've learned, over time, to access my greatest strengths. My ability to park is a happy coincidence. My ability to drive has become a taproot for the character of the woman I have become.

BE FIERCE

What is your writing superpower? What is your kryptonite? How do you think your kryptonite has shaped your sense of purpose, discipline, or expectation? And how do the two weave together in practice as you live and write with intention?

BE GRATEFUL

I used to think of gratitude as a spontaneous response to good things that happened. In recent years, however, I have come to understand that gratitude is much more than an automatic by-product of positive experience. Gratitude can actually be an emotional and intellectual baseline, if we so choose.

What I mean is that we don't have to wait around for good things to happen in order to feel grateful. We can simply find things to be grateful for no matter what happens or how far afield we may be from what we desire. From this vantage point, everything we experience gives us something to appreciate, no matter how difficult or seemingly inconsequential it might be.

I saw this concept modeled recently by a workshop leader who pretended to smash his thumb with a hammer. After shouting bloody murder, he said, "Boy, am I glad that doesn't happen very often." And then, "Wow, check out all of that sensation in my thumb! I'm so glad I have nerves to tell me that I have injured myself."

It is uncommon to interpret an unfortunate event with gratitude. But this man demonstrated that doing so is always an option. When you find ways to appreciate a difficult experience—or at least use it to appreciate how great your life was before and after it happened—you set yourself up to feel empowered. *You* get to decide how events in your life—both good and bad—affect you.

My first memory of choosing gratitude over, say, revenge was in college. I had broken up with my first love, and the emotional pain was so intense that I feared it would kill me. A few weeks later, when I knew conclusively that my body would keep going no matter how sad I was, I focused on the thrill of being alive. If I had survived this heartbreak,

I could expect to survive the losses of future loves to come. This was good news! When I shifted my gaze from pain to gratitude, I stumbled into discovery.

This early loss helped me trust that I could weather the disappointments of my literary life as well. Over the years, I have come to appreciate each publication that rejected my work for the opportunity it provided to work harder, write better, and find a truer fit for my work. And I have deeply appreciated the teachers, editors, colleagues, and writing group friends who have given me uncomfortable feedback that has challenged me to grow.

In every so-called mistake, failure, and disappointment, I have been further refined as a writer and a person. I have so much to appreciate.

Of course, every day of our writing lives, endless things also go right. Choosing gratitude doesn't just help us transcend our bad fortune. It also helps us integrate our good fortune. Gratitude is just as important—and just as easy to overlook—when things are going well as when they're not.

When you acknowledge yourself for how hard you're working, it can make a significant difference in your endurance and your mood. When you show up at your writing desk at the time you promised yourself; when you move through the angst of the blank page; when you complete the first draft, the revision, and the next revision; when you are willing to get feedback from your writing group; when you have the fortitude to research submissions; when you muster the courage to submit and resubmit your work—these are all opportunities to appreciate yourself. When you notice and acknowledge how capable and courageous you are, you anchor this in your being. You start to learn that you can count on yourself. Whether or not you ultimately achieve the result you want, you have numerous successes to refer to that can help you more deeply receive your epic wins, or more effectively redirect your efforts to try again.

A writer friend told me that after the release of his first book, he sent out a wave of thank-you letters and e-mails to all the people who had influenced his thinking and writing. Only after he had expressed his appreciation did he launch into marketing and press outreach. He explained that framing the whole experience in gratitude reduced his anxiety about whether the book would sell and changed his approach completely.

Gratitude anchored him in the field of influence from which his book was called into existence, and it kept his focus on the service his book was offering. This quickly put his book in the hands of a global community seeking his wisdom.

When we focus on problems, we generate dissatisfaction and resentment. When we invest in fears, we can destabilize ourselves. But when gratitude is the ground on which we stand, we can be satisfied with life exactly as it is and relax into the unknown, while becoming more receptive to all that we desire.

BE SLOW

During an E. coli outbreak in prepackaged fresh spinach a decade ago, Susie Bright shared a story by Andy Griffin of Mariquita Farms on her blog. Griffin proposed that it is not the spinach that makes us vulnerable to viruses such as e-coli, but our processing and packaging systems, driven by our mass-distribution demands and the ever-escalating expectations of consumer convenience. He observed:

> A psychologist might be able to do a better job than I in telling you why so many people feel comforted when they see their food coming to them in sterile-looking sealed plastic bags covered in corporate logos, nutritional information, legal disclaimers and "use by" dates … . But I'll tell you that every sealed bag of pre-washed greens is like a little green house. The greens inside are still alive, as are the bacteria living on them. If the produce in the bag is clean, great, but if it isn't the bacteria present has a wonderful little sealed environment to reproduce in, free from any threat until the dressing splashes down and the shadow of a fork passes over. Frankly, I think convenience is overrated.

Griffin's words woke me up to the truth that convenience can kill, and I started noticing that, in my own life, speed and convenience were like the snake eating its tail. The more overwhelmed I became by my various commitments, the more I felt that certain parts of my life needed to be less labor intensive. To give more time to my writing, the rest of my life had become a routinized blur of feeding, grooming, driving, and working to fuel the machine of productivity. But to what end?

As it turned out, efficiency and creativity were at odds. When the rest of my life lacked presence, so did my writing. Rushing blindly through one part of my day didn't prepare me well for a spacious and receptive experience when it was time to write. Convenience wasn't literally killing me, but it was quietly choking out the consciousness in which my best writing happens.

The ultimate convenience for me was my car, so I stopped driving for a month. On foot and on bike, I slowed down and woke up. Every errand was automatically invigorating, because I relied solely on physical movement for transportation. And by moving slowly enough to take in the view, I felt more grounded in my neighborhood and more present in my life.

On a long walk to a meeting where I was going to reconcile a difficult choice I had made in the past, I spotted a torn piece of notebook paper on the sidewalk. I paused, turned around, and picked it up. In bubble letters drawn in pencil someone had written, "Can't take back the things I've done before." That note felt like a divine intervention. It connected me to all people of all ages who struggle to reconcile their choices and their actions by writing them down and then letting them go. That note lived on my bulletin board for years. It reminded me that when we are slow enough to pay attention, we generate the kind of vision that can transform litter into gift.

During my "slow month," I joined a community-supported agriculture (CSA) group, where I paid for a farm share and received local, seasonal produce directly from a farm in my community. Now, as a CSA member, I participate in what feels like a secret society of righteous eating. On Wednesday evenings, I show up at a neighbor's garage, where a bounty of vegetables is spread out for members. I often think of Thomas Pynchon's *The Crying of Lot 49*, in which the protagonist stumbles into a worldwide conspiracy that involves an underground postal service. The shock I felt while reading about a viable alternative to the USPS was akin to the thrill I feel every time I collect my produce directly from the people who have grown it.

Supporting a local farm that grows the most gorgeous and delicious vegetables I have ever eaten has changed my relationship with convenience. I show up to collect my produce when I am told; I take home whatever I am given; and I feed myself in a way that makes me feel connected to the land I live on, engaged with my neighbors who share my gratitude for this bounty, and blessed to have so many choices about how to feed and sustain this great mystery that is my life. I have come to feel the same way about writing. Being slow has changed the conversation entirely from what I am accomplishing to what I am noticing. The quality of my attention defines the quality of my work and my life.

I show up, receive whatever I am given, and use it to quench the thirst that keeps me in service to the page, the stanza, the line, the word.

INHABIT THE UNIVERSAL

During the month when I had planned to start writing my first nonfiction book, I watched all five seasons of *Six Feet Under* instead. Spending fifty or so hours steeped in the daily deaths and dramas of the Fisher family seemed to be my most effective procrastination strategy ever.

I was acutely aware, of course, that I was wasting time. But what I didn't understand then was that I was priming myself for the next eight months of fierce writing by inhabiting stories that profoundly awakened me to myself. Which makes me suspect that I mistook procrastination for incubation—the vital generative writing stage explored in chapter twenty-nine. As uncomfortable as it was to admit, I identified deeply with every main character in the series: the dead father, whose ghost visited biting judgment upon the family he left behind, his disoriented widow, the prodigal son and his unpredictable girlfriend, the teenage daughter thrashing about in search of identity, and the gay younger brother who assumed the mantle of managing the family funeral home.

Through the show's endless deaths and discoveries, plot turns, heartbreaks, and healings, I was brought more acutely to the edge of my own humanity. Story was firing in my every cell. I was living six lives beyond my own. Through these invented people and the exquisitely executed story that wove us all together, I awakened to new dimensions of the human experience.

I can see now that *Six Feet Under* was the channel that gave me a direct line to a second huge and timeless life beyond my own, one that mirrored invigorating insights. This is our opportunity and privilege as writers: to tell stories that give us greater access to ourselves and to each other. The more we attune ourselves to the stories we experience, and the more we seek out the ones that we are compelled to grapple with, the more fertile the soil of our own creations.

The writing life is the great cosmic blackboard upon which we revise and reinvent all that has already been thought, lived, and written into legends of our own invention.

Kevin Van Valkenburg, senior writer for ESPN, says, "It's human nature to want to explain the universe, and to do that right, you need to see the world through other people's eyes." He pursues this type of vision as a journalist. I often seek it out as a poet and an essayist. You may penetrate the human condition through fiction or screenplays or love letters or monologues. Each of us, through the genres we are drawn to and offerings we are called to make, finds our own way to stretch beyond our individual reach into something deeper and wider that we all share.

What I learned from my deep dive into *Six Feet Under* is that, as a writer, I have an opportunity, maybe even a responsibility, to see myself in everything. To claim my place in the universal, I must understand that the marathoner who crosses the finish line with no hands or feet is a part of my story—the hard breaths of determination she draws in those final miles also pummel my lungs. The child who trades her Halloween candy for an American Girl doll and realizes too late that she was unprepared to relinquish her Kit-Kat bars shares my hunger for sweetness. The dead and the dying, the lost and the found all have stories to tell that inform my own.

Writing initiates us into the universal. We align ourselves with the currents of human experience and wash up on the riverbanks of exodus, homecoming, and everything in between. All truth, all invention, all that has been said and done and imagined runs through all of us. When we allow ourselves to receive it, we are better equipped to write it.

The paradox is that by inhabiting and inventing the lives of others, we inherit ourselves.

DON'T RUSH THE ENDING

At the book launch celebration for the short story anthology *The Night, and the Rain, and the River,* editor Liz Prato was asked what makes a good ending. Liz explained that she teaches a craft class on ways to begin a story, but that each story needs to find its own ending. And she emphasized how difficult this can be.

I hold myself up as an example of this difficulty. When I submitted my story for the anthology, it was Liz who gently pointed out that the piece didn't quite end. I was exploring an unresolved dynamic between two people, and I wasn't sure how to depict this lack of closure while actually closing the story. The beauty of a great editor is that she can offer friendly encouragement from a bit farther down the road and awaken you to the distance you have yet to travel.

As writers, we are given the infinitely interesting task of deciding how to hand the story off to readers in a way that lets them come to their own conclusions. And we need to leave them at a place resonant enough to compel them to do so.

The short story that Liz helped me complete took somewhere between ten and fifteen years for me to write. I had to grow up enough to understand the consequences of the choices my young characters were making. I needed to stretch my own perspective further than theirs so I could shine a light from the other side. This is how stories, poems, and essays have been my greatest teachers. It is literature that sends out its lifeboats into the abyss of the unknown. It is writing that gives us the illusion that we are getting some traction there. It is words that cushion our fall.

The entire story finally settled into itself when I found a way to leave the door of the piece ajar for readers to stand in its last beams of escaping light. This is that moment I write for: when the language and emotion and narrative all transcend their individual labors and, for a brief moment, sing.

But maybe even more important, I write to keep myself company in those moments, years, and decades when nothing sings.

There is no resonance like meeting oneself on the page as we track the story to its end, let the great, eternal middle of our writing lives be resplendent in messes, and then join the current of story that runs through each of us on its way to the great waters.

Stories teach us when it's time to end, but more often they insist that we keep on going. Ever since I wrote my first expository essay in high school, I have gravitated to the resolution of tidy endings that circle back to some bit of wisdom and gratitude. It was a shock at age forty, during the anguish of my divorce, that I could not bring any piece of writing to conclusion or certainty. It felt like I was simply writing myself off a cliff with each poem and essay I attempted. I discovered then that leaving a frayed end of a story open and raw was sometimes the only true choice.

I also came to understand that if you're not satisfied with the ending, you can simply keep writing. As long as you are still alive, you have an opportunity to revise both your writing and your life circumstance. There is so much we can't know until we know it. If you've come to a dead-end, try another path.

Just remember: Each time you write yourself off a cliff, you get to decide how you land.

POETIC LICENSE GRANTED

Years ago, I took a workshop with the author Susan Wooldridge, during which she handed out driver's license-size cards that said "Poetic License." I thought this was brilliant. We all crave permission—poetic license—to be ourselves, in our writing and in our lives. And this was a fun way to invite us to claim it.

I thought of this card when I received a note from a writer whom I'd never met. She was taking a class on the business of writing, but instead of helping clarify her path, the class had confused her and shut her down. This brought to mind the endless confessions I hear from writers when I teach, speak, and blog about how they've tried to create support for themselves in ways that have backfired.

Writers everywhere are feeling misunderstood and alienated in their writing groups, completely unable to write the novel they believe they should be writing (and therefore writing nothing) or struggling to make sense of feedback from teachers or other "experts" that doesn't resonate and gets them tangled up in a bad feeling with no resolution. I'll bet you could cite something off the top of your head to add to this list.

The irony is that often the very pursuit of support interferes with our writing.

Occasionally, I swoop in to extricate one of my cats from what started as a wonderful stretch and ended in a panicked, hanging-from-the-couch-by-a-claw dangle. As I see it, poetic license is the superhero ability to do this for ourselves: to see where we are stuck and take swift action to release.

What would this look like? Here are a few possibilities: If a class you're taking is shutting you down, enroll in a different one. If your writing group is not providing information and inspiration, it might not be the one for you. If you force yourself to outline your plot because you read that doing so is more efficient than pantsing your way through—even though you know this method won't hold your interest enough to keep you motivated—consider sticking with your natural tendency. And if you're writing short stories today, don't let the expectation that you'll write a novel someday distract you from the work at hand.

A student of mine writes beautiful stories and poems. She works hard at her craft—and at finding the right context in which to keep herself moving forward. Recently, she started a blog to celebrate two areas of expertise (gardening and cooking) that also happen to be two business services she offers. Practically overnight, she became thrilled with her writing process, and the spirit and quality of her writing reflects this. This writer has found a point of entry—in both form and content—that makes her feel not just invested but exhilarated to show up at the page. (I should point out that she started blogging only after ensuring, through self-reflection, that she had plenty of ideas for posts and a passion to bring them forth on a regular basis. She didn't want to set herself up for an expectation she wasn't likely to fulfill.)

If your writing path is littered with roadblocks, I invite you to grant yourself poetic license to simply try something else. Chances are good that you've made a well-meaning commitment that has outlived its usefulness—or was never useful in the first place.

Poetic license is your unique ability to seek and define your writing sweet spot. It's your permission slip to ignore input that does not propel you forward and to fully inhabit all that does.

BE FIERCE

What can you give yourself poetic license to stop doing or start doing that will help you regain your momentum? What "good advice" or "useful feedback" would be better ignored? What secret part of you needs permission to exist, to try, to mess it all up, and to keep going?

WHAT IF MARHETING WERE LOVE MADE CONTAGIOUS?

When Theo was three, I once folded his monthly preschool payment into a poem I had written recently—about Theo and stars and divorce and transformation—before placing both in the envelope for the preschool director. In this simple and impulsive act, my poet, mother, and professional marketing selves experienced a kind of harmonic convergence. I felt wholeness in sharing the right offering, from the deepest well of my soul, with a person likely to welcome it.

It struck me that the concept behind marketing is as simple as this.

We all get the delighted impulse to share. When you offer something that has personal meaning or value to an audience whose interests are concentric to yours, this invites them to enjoy and embrace what you love. Announcing a reading or teaching gig, sharing publication news, or offering links to or copies of your poems and prose can all be communicated in this spirit, from that powerful, tender, and wide-open place that called forth the work.

So many of us feel awkward, ashamed, false, or inept when it comes time to bring the privacy of our work into a brighter public light. You might imagine that others who share themselves are more accomplished or confident than you.

But what if you let go completely of the idea that you need a certain amount of bluster or bravado to promote yourself? Instead, consider how you could let what you love most about your intimate writing life ripple out to the people around you.

This year, when I continued the payment-in-poem tradition at Theo's new school, one of the school's founders, who loves poetry, sought me out to talk about it. As this conversation evolved through the school year, we decided that I would offer a poetry class as an elective for the older students.

This is what can happen when you make your passion visible. You become magnetic to others who love what you love—or who may be ready to consider exploring it for the first time. You weave the fabric of your life together more intentionally with others who share what you value. And you make greater and more meaningful contributions, because people know and appreciate what you have to offer.

I enjoy enclosing the preschool payment with a poem so much that I am now considering sending my utility bill payments in the same way. Not because I want Portland General Electric to buy my book or to read my blog, but because it feels good to give thanks with what I have to give: poems. Thank you, PGE, for making it possible for me to use this computer. In exchange, here is a poem that makes it possible for me to inhabit my humanity more completely. In making this offering, I affirm my place in the life poetic and keep the channels of generosity and receptivity open.

BE FIERCE

You probably don't feel apprehensive about sharing a spoonful of a delicious dessert with a friend. What if you approached marketing your writing with the exact same impulse? What do you have to give today just because it feels good to do so? I propose that your passion, unburdened by judgment and fear, will be contagious.

THE GLINT OF LIGHT ON BROKEN GLASS

DON'T TELL ME THE MOON IS SHINING; SHOW ME THE GLINT OF LIGHT ON BROKEN GLASS. —*Anton Chekhov*

When I lived in San Francisco in my midtwenties, one of my good friends from college, Josh, came to visit. We spent a day at the Exploratorium, a hands-on museum of arts and sciences. There we played a game in which we sat with a divider between us, each equipped with matching sets of colored blocks of varying shapes and sizes. One person would build something with the blocks and then describe it to the other person, who would attempt to build a replication based on the instructions given by the builder.

I was the builder first, and Josh interpreted my instructions into form. The task seemed simple enough as I made a little block temple and then began to explain how to replicate it. But it didn't turn out to be simple at all. When I finished giving my instructions and Josh finished building, we removed the divider to compare our work. Josh's interpretation didn't match my building in the slightest. When we reversed roles, we had the same experience.

I was astonished to discover that Josh and I, two friends of comparable intelligence, education, context, and mind-set, saw our environment and communicated what we saw so differently. This insight became one of the anchors of my writing practice.

I concluded that the point isn't to see the same as everyone else, or even to help everyone see what we see, which is impossible anyway.

The writer's opportunity is to present our version of the world—the one we report on, or the one we invent—with such great detail that it gives our readers greater access to their own experience.

Consider these possibilities for giving your writing the fierce specificity that creates liftoff:

1. **SHOW AND TELL**: Make imagery and explanation work powerfully together to evoke vivid scenes and instruct the reader about their meaning. Consider whether your work would be better served by writing "The sky is ominous" or "The sky is a eulogy" rather than "The sky is gray" or "The sky looks bleak."

2. **LET VOICE BE AUTHENTIC**: Use words that express the narrator's or characters' temperament, context, and predicament. How would word choice affect the dialogue of a child calling to a friend on the playground? How does this compare to the words of a man speaking to his wife from his deathbed?

3. **MAKE EVERY WORD COUNT**: Seek maximum potency in the language you choose. Consider whether there's a more impactful way to convey a thought, feeling, or idea. Can passive verbs become active? Can modifiers be cut? Should *dropped* be changed to *plummeted*?

4. **BRING IN THE BODY**: Engage your readers' senses by crafting a tangible world for them to taste, feel, see, and hear. Is "I am lonely" more palpable as "I know the metal taste of alone"?

5. **GROUND IT WITH SOUND**: Create tones that echo the story's emotions and action. Repeating sounds create unity and music. Consider this sentence: "*It is hard to know how to let go.*" How does the repeating *o* sounds in this line bring a melancholy and rhythm that underscores its meaning?

6. **OWN THE PACING**: Construct the rhythm of language and pacing of sentences and paragraphs to control the reader's movement through the story. Should tension or speed be conveyed in choppy sentences and languor in lengthy ones?

7. **LET THE WORLD IN**: Illuminate the emotional world of your characters with the physical world and its lighting, weather, and street noise.

8. **TELL THE TRUTH**: Discover what is emotionally true in your writing and strive to let it rise like steam from your well-prepared meal.

9. **SHAKE THINGS UP**: Never stop experimenting with ways to make language serve your story. Try paring down a narrative to give it energy or tension. Swap out dialogue for exposition to launch a scene. Do the opposite of what you are typically inclined to do, and see what happens.

10. **FEEL THE FEAR AND DO IT ANYWAY**: The fierce writer persists.

You could tell us the pie Savannah served was delicious. Or you could show us the jeans you unbuttoned to make room for more. Include us in what compelled you to drive ninety miles to arrive at Savannah's kitchen in time for dessert—and how the grit on your tongue mingles with the powdered sugar.

Accuracy is impossible, because we all bring our own lens to any experience and construct our own towers of insight. But *specificity* is glorious. By showing the reader a vivid and palpable way into a piece of writing, we help them commit physically and emotionally to take the ride with us.

Go as deep as you can go into the subjective (either yours or your character's), and your readers will follow you anywhere.

OBSERVATION AS TRANSPORTATION

My adult life contains two parallel quests: to write well and to live well. In the last decade, I have come to understand that these paths are inextricably intertwined such that writing well has revealed the path toward living well. For many of us, writing is an accidental path toward healing, but it also can be an intentional restorative tool. We can write ourselves through great difficulty, and we can also write as a proactive way to cultivate well-being.

Getting curious about your pain can be a powerful way to transform it. A writing practice can give you firm footing in the neutral middle ground of observation. When you are simply curious, you can diffuse the stories of blame, shame, and regret you tell yourself and let go of your attachment to a particular outcome. This is a generous place to stand, both with yourself and with others.

Through writing, you can train yourself to be present with discomfort and simply record it as if you were studying a thunderstorm. As you observe what is, you can actually move toward the pain. Why in the world would anyone want to do that? Because at the center of what hurts the most is the greatest gift: the undisclosed insight you have not yet learned to mine.

It is human nature to want to resolve pain as quickly as possible. But I have learned that simply studying pain, in writing, can be the most powerful and efficient way to heal deeply and to make huge paradigm shifts. As you write, you are teaching yourself that you can tolerate your own truths, that you are safe with them.

Leonard Cohen says, "There is a crack in everything. That's how the light gets in." Writers have an opportunity to tend these broken places with words so we can mine the lessons, the wisdom, the gifts, and the grace.

It was my poetry practice that got me through the first two-and-a-half years of Theo's life. Every two hours of every night, he was awake—and I was awake with him. As I rocked, sang, and read to him, I steered my thoughts away from the repetitive misery of my exhaustion and instead simply paid attention.

I steeped in our late-night silence and found words to describe the light in the room, the smell of my child's head, and the vulnerability of my depleted body. I became a third-person observer. Through this lens of heightened objectivity, I was astonished by the fierce power of this woman rocking in the soft green chair and equally astonished by the impossible beauty of her child.

Some nights, I'd tune into the universal, knowing that women all over the world were awake in this very moment, as exhausted and miserable and euphoric and wild with love for their wide-awake babies as I was. I could feel the chorus of our bodies and our songs; I was captivated by this web of life and tradition. I placed myself in its deep sense of belonging through the quality of my attention. It was all I had.

Thanks to poetry, I could tune in to something deeper, wider, and larger than my small self and my small moment. By being curious and paying attention, I moved through some of my least resourced moments in a way that initiated me into motherhood more deeply.

A few years later, when I was entering my divorce years, I started an alphabet-based project called the Rage Diaries, a collection of essays from A to Z. Every night I wrote a brief rage explosion on whatever topic wanted to rise up. I wrote pieces titled "C is for Coyote" and "S is for Stomach" and felt as if I was stringing together a necklace of grenades. The random structure gave me an organizing principle loose enough to follow my grief through its endless associations.

These essays were like nothing I had ever penned before. The words were like blades moving clean through the paper.

In a short time, I had completed twenty-six essays that gave my heartbreak a wide palate of expression. I felt as if I had been wringing out a wet towel for hours while standing in a downpour. I was exhausted, purified, burned to the wick's end.

The Chinese symbol for *"crisis"* is composed of the symbols for *danger* and *opportunity*. I think of this symbol as a writer's totem, one that can move us through pain into a new place. At a time of crisis, simply observing "what is" in writing can become a kind of transportation from danger to opportunity. Once you have written to the end of emotion, you are in a much better position to understand the choices you have about what to say next.

BE FIERCE

The next time you're struggling with a problem that you're not sure how to solve, consider giving it your full attention through your writing. Notice what happens when you study yourself and your difficulty as though you are a third-person observer. How do you see connections to other moments in your life or the lives around you? Is there something quieter, gentler, and more true in the eye of your storm than you ever could have reached without writing yourself to this place?

STOP SMUSHING BANANAS

At the age of three, Theo understood that if he offered a reason, it could excuse him from having to do something—or at least buy him time. One morning as we sat together eating breakfast, for example, I asked him to stop smushing banana into my arm. He replied, "But I'm too sad to stop smushing banana."

See what I mean?

Recently I caught myself in what I now call a "too sad to stop smushing bananas" loop. In short, I had a good excuse for why I was stuck, miserable, and floundering, and it had as much to do with my capacity to get things done as happiness has with banana smushing.

That Mommy voice inside of me stepped in with the voice of reason. "You can be sad *and* stop smushing banana at the same time," it said. "And that's what I am asking you to do now."

Thank you, Mommy voice, for reminding me that at any moment, we can stop telling ourselves we can't and instead simply do what needs to be done.

Faced with an impossibly busy week, I put this principle to the test. I had twelve hours of client work to complete each day, and my child was in preschool for only six hours. This meant that a good part of my workday happened in the middle of the night. It occurred to me for the first time that juggling a variety of client projects as a consultant is very much like having five children with overlapping emergencies, needs, demands, and interpersonal challenges.

"You can be exhausted, hopeless, and overwhelmed, *and* you can stop smushing bananas at the same time," said the Mommy voice.

I decided to focus on what felt within reach.

I fed and bathed and played with my child, drove him back and forth to school, and finished my client work well and on time. I walked my dogs and took one to the veterinarian.

How did the writing life hold up for this single parent supporting a family? By a spider's thread: invisible, but strong and deeply connected to the margins of everything. I updated my writing to-do list so that once I actually had the luxury of time to sit at my desk and write something, I'd immediately know my highest priority. I tidied up my piles of unsorted paper so they wouldn't distract me when I entered my office. I also wrote down every administrative task I needed to accomplish—several pages worth—for the coming months so those logistics could stop jangling around inside my head. By tidying up my interior and exterior spaces, I made space for creative rumination.

And, as an experiment, I asked my subconscious to do some of the heavy creative lifting as I slept. As a result, several dreams informed my sense of direction for my writing. Every time I wandered into grumpiness or started to feel like a victim, I took a step back to remind myself that successful client work equaled food, clothing, and housing for my family and me.

Creative writing accomplished? No. Creative foundation reinforced? Yes.

This much, for that week, was triumph.

I was reminded that when you can't act, planning can be both a satisfying and productive substitute. Can't write for two hours? Spend two minutes imagining and outlining what you will accomplish during your next two-hour session; this sets the session in motion long before you put your butt in the chair. Dream about it. Hold it in a designated place in your mind while you are committed to thinking about other things. Be curious, be sloppy, be exhausted and defeated if you need to be, but understand that even in this moment you have options.

Smush or don't smush bananas as you like, but don't stop appreciating and spinning the invisible web of your writing life, which is strung one intention, one action at a time, deeper and deeper into the impossible.

BE FIERCE

What are you telling yourself you can't get done in your writing life right now? How does this make you feel? What if you could take one simple next step? What would that step be? If you can't act, what can you plan instead? How can you appreciate yourself for all you are doing to support and nourish your creative foundation—no matter what else you must make happen in your life?

REACHING HIGH
IS THE TRUE TRIUMPH

Early in high school, I became infatuated with Bobby Sullivan. He was in my gym class, which was a forty-minute reprieve from the caste divides of teenage social order: the smart kids, the popular kids, the stoners, the Goody Two-Shoes. Bobby was kind in an enigmatic sort of way, and he had those sad, looking-beyond-me eyes that would become my holy grail of fumbled romance for many years to come. Everyone knew that the people you talked to in gym class weren't the people you talked to in the halls—when you had on your real clothes and your real friends were in reach.

For a week or two, I biked past Bobby's house in Woodcrest every day after school, back and forth, back and forth, as the leaves papered the streets. I don't know what I thought would happen if he actually came out and saw me, but I had no other choice but to continue circling. I'd been sucked into this boy's orbit. I needed something from him that I couldn't understand.

When it became clear that my bike tires could not impress my yearning for Bobby into the pavement around his house, I rode home. I became shy and strange in gym class. And then I made a decision: I would tell Bobby the truth. I had to unburden myself of its weight. I wrote this boy a letter.

The words knew what they wanted to say. I wrote and when I was finished, I carefully folded the notebook paper and shoved it at him one afternoon, overcome with hope and shame, as we headed into the halls of our respective identities.

Bobby never mentioned the letter.

Though even as I wrote the letter I was fairly certain my feelings would not be reciprocated, being entirely ignored felt awful. But that is only part of the story. Underneath the burning embarrassment was a more settled feeling of what, in retrospect, could only be called triumph. I had been brave. I had something to share, and I shared it. And in doing so, I was released from my compulsive need for reciprocation. Just owning what was true for myself—and reaching for it—was enough.

This is my first memory of becoming aware of the pleasure of "going for it," a feeling distinct and independent from "getting it." I told myself that now I didn't have to wonder what could be possible with Bobby. I had done my part and gotten my answer in his nonanswer. Now I could move on.

A decade later, in a city across the country from our south Jersey high school, Bobby (who now went by Bob) was dating a friend of mine, someone else from high school who had not been in my social caste. I don't know how it happened, but somehow, in this new early-adult context, we were all friends.

One day, out of the blue, Bob thanked me for my letter. He told me that its honesty and straightforwardness had terrified him at the time, that he had been far too immature to know how to respond, and that he had always been ashamed of his lack of courage when I had taken such a risk. I was both surprised and moved to hear that my letter had affected him at all. And I was reminded that even when you don't get what you want, you can never presume to know why other people do what they do (or don't do).

I think of Bobby when I need to remember that it's okay to be clear about what I want, even if I'm not likely to get it. In fact, I have come to believe that it is not just okay but essential to my happiness. It's a rather efficient process, if you think about it. Had I not written Bobby that letter, I might still be circling his house on my ten-speed. Instead, I got my answer from him and moved on to my next crush, James Gallagher, who pulled arrows out of my chest in a dream shortly thereafter.

I have come to appreciate reaching and missing as the best kind of psychosocial yoga. Few people agree with me: Seth Godin suggests that we let go of expectation, while Pema Chódrón advises that we give up hope. But I think *not* expecting and *not* hoping makes things pretty darn confusing. If you don't know where you're headed, how can you know when you have arrived? In my experience, the most pleasurable part of moving toward a goal is the *moving toward* part.

The sticky part for us humans is how bad we can feel if and when we don't arrive.

I didn't get Bobby the boyfriend, but I got Bob the friend—it just took us a decade to get there. But *really* what I got when I wrote that letter was my first glimpse of myself as a woman of clarity, a woman of truth, a woman who could live with *no* for an answer and even be satisfied with no answer at all.

BE FIERCE

Submitting writing for publication is an act of great hope and vulnerability. We set our sights, we take a risk, and we don't know what will happen next. What if you considered dropping your carefully prepared envelope in the mailbox (or clicking "submit" on Submittable) as the triumph, and anything that came after that as the gravy? What if rejection were an opportunity to seek another publication that is better suited for you in this moment? Or what if it revealed an opportunity for revision that you didn't see before?

Facing the unknowns of the submission process can refine us as people and writers. Accepting the feedback we get as an opportunity to grow cultivates our humility. Knowing we can count on ourselves to take risks that move us forward can change the course of our lives—and our work.

NOTICE, INTEND, ACT.

As far as I can tell, intention is the most powerful and mysterious treasure map that exists. Clarifying what you want in the future starts with understanding and appreciating where you are, who you are, and what you're doing right now. So I invite you to start paying attention to and answering questions such as these for yourself.

- What is my writing rhythm lately? How frequently do I write, for what duration, at what times?
- Is this rhythm working for me? Am I enjoying it, producing as much as I want, writing at the optimal hours, and so on?
- What am I reading? How is it serving or not serving me?
- How do my sleeping, eating, socializing, imbibing, social networking, and exercising choices impact my writing?
- How do my family life, work life, and community life impact my writing?
- What makes me want to sit down and write? And what keeps me there?
- When do I avoid doing the writing I intend to do?
- What do I love about writing?
- What do I struggle with?
- How do I know when I'm in the sweet spot with a piece of writing?
- How do I decide when to edit and when to stop editing?
- Who is in my writing life right now? Friends, teachers, editors, writing group members?
  - What am I grateful to them for?
  - Are they a fit for me? Am I energized and inspired by their company?

- Do they give me the kind of support, feedback, and camaraderie I want and need?
- What am I working on that pleases me?
- What can't I seem to finish?
- What do people tell me about my writing that seems accurate?
- What do I believe about my writing life?
- What writers, books, and writing do I admire?
- What do I admire most about my own writing?
- What do I appreciate most about how I conduct my writing life?
- Are certain habits, fears, or beliefs limiting my ability to write in the way that I would like?
- What am I grateful for in my writing life?
- How have I written, submitted for publication, or published in accordance with my goals this year?
- How would I describe my writing in one to two sentences?
- What did I learn about myself as a writer, or about writing in general, this year?
- Whose books seem like they are in the same family as my work?

Write down answers to the questions that speak to you, or come up with your own inquiries about who you are as a writer today. However you choose to go about it, my hope is that you will spend some time observing your writing life.

Once you have a composite of who you are today, consider what kind of writing life you *want* moving forward.

- What kind of writing rhythm do I want?
- What do I want to read?
- How do I want to sleep, eat, socialize, imbibe, and exercise to influence my writing?
- How do I want my family life, work life, and community life to impact my writing?
- How can I keep my butt in the chair to write?
- How can I enjoy my writing process more?
- What do I want to stop struggling with?
- How can I stay in the sweet spot with a piece of writing?

- How can I most effectively edit and stop editing?
- Whom do I want in my writing life?
- What could I work on that would please me?
- How can I finish what is unfinished?
- What do I want to be known for in my writing life?
- What do I want to believe about my writing life?
- What do I want to admire most about my writing?
- What habits, fears, or beliefs do I want to change?
- How can I be more grateful in my writing life?
- How could I better write, submit for publication, or publish in accordance with my goals?
- How would I describe what I am striving for in my writing in one to two sentences?
- What do I want to discover about myself as a writer, or about writing in general, this year?

When you know what you want and pay attention to the choices you make, you can discover how your actions and desires are aligned—or out of alignment. With clarity, you can make choices about adjusting your practices so that they move you toward what you want to do, be, and have.

IF EVERYONE ELSE WAS JUMPING OFF A BRIDGE

I'm sure you are familiar with this popular parent-child debate about group mentality:

KID: "But Mom, all the other kids are doing it!"
MOM: "If all the other kids were jumping off a bridge, would you jump, too?"

Of course, this is not a question meant to invite an answer but to interrupt an unreasonable request with the kind of logic that evades most children. What moms are missing in our grown-up rationale is this: *Yes*, kids would most likely jump off a bridge if everyone else was doing it. That's just human nature. Whether it's a good idea matters far less than the pull of the community and the choices they are making. And adults are equally likely to jump when they see *their* peers jumping.

A friend recently shared the "no you may not" comeback she uses with her kids, which seems a bit more to the point and contains no loopholes: "Because I'm the mother, and this isn't a democracy." But I digress.

In 1999, when a handful of young, aspiring novelists decided to spend the month of November completing a novel-writing marathon, they translated the age-old adage "jump when others are jumping" into "write when others are writing." So effective was their message that it has snowballed into a well-known movement: National Novel Writing Month (NaNoWriMo). This movement has since led to NaPoWriMo (National Poetry Writing Month), held in April.

If this kind of epic writing fest is right up your alley, you have probably already plugged in. Likewise, if it's definitely not your thing, you've probably tuned it out. But many of us occupy a middle ground. Perhaps it's simply not realistic for you to dedicate such an enormous amount of consecutive time to your craft. Or you might have too many conflicting commitments during the designated NaNoWriMo month. Or maybe you don't have a project in the works that warrants this kind of attention.

Because I get an energetic boost just imagining writers and poets all over the country committing to their practice on this shared adventure, I'm curious if there is a middle way to participate, one that invites us to ride the energy wave of November or April with more modest expectations of our output. Something equivalent to skipping over the bridge, or standing next to the bridge and studying jumping techniques, or jumping on a trampoline instead.

If you're feeling totally in sync with all the other poets or writers during NaPoWriMo and NaNoWriMo, fabulous! And if you're not, I invite you to experiment with riding the wave of momentum in your own way, one that is authentic to who you are, what you want to accomplish, and the margins you can realistically afford to create for your writing.

When Theo was four years old and NaPoWriMo was just around the corner, I was writing so much for clients and sleeping so little that just moving my hands and arms felt painful and slow. I decided that, at most, I could carve out one hour for writing every day for a month. I promised myself that I would dedicate that daily hour throughout the month of April to write for my own pleasure, even if I had to wake up in the middle of the night to do it. Period.

In that month, I somehow applied the right amount of pressure to show up at the page, combined with the permission not to produce anything in particular. As a result, almost an entire volume of first-draft poems poured through me. Some I finished and published quickly. Others I've been refining and reimagining ever since. But what became of those poems is less significant than the fact that I'd found a way to ride the slipstream of a collective, national effort to write. And in doing so, a goal I wouldn't have dreamed possible thirty days earlier became reality.

Yes, I jumped off the bridge because everyone else was doing it—and because moving forward in good company is one of the most efficient and enjoyable ways to meet my own goals. Besides, I'm the mom, and this is not a democracy.

BE FIERCE

What if you committed yourself to a MyProWriMo (My Promise to Write Month—or Week, or Weekend, or Tuesday Night)? Make sure your promise is aspirational but also within reach. It could align with all of the great writing momentum of NaNoWriMo or NaPoWriMo, or it could help you establish and sustain a rhythm that is all your own.

THE TRAFFIC CONE AND THE UNDER-CONSTRUCTION WRITING LIFE

One morning as Theo and I headed out for preschool, we encountered a beat-up orange traffic cone on our front stoop. It was a strange thing to find. It was even stranger to imagine that someone had walked all the way up to the front door to place it there, for reasons I couldn't fathom.

I moved the cone to the grass strip between the sidewalk and the street, hoping that it whoever had left it there would collect it. No such luck. After a few days, during which the cone sat resolutely in front of our house, I moved it to the driveway, where it stood for several weeks, alerting passersby to I'm not sure what.

Every time I saw the cone I didn't quite feel responsible for and couldn't seem to properly dispose of, it brought to mind all the gray areas in my life: the self-care I intended but wasn't getting around to, the limiting stories I told myself, the administrative tasks, such as returning the too-small boots and too-small curtains, that seemed too hard to deal with.

In the few short weeks of our strange acquaintance, that cone came to brightly symbolize all of my immobilized places.

The traffic cone is an interesting symbol, because it calls attention to a problem while also offering encouragement that the problem will be addressed if you just stay out of the way long enough. The cone's solemn and mute visitation made me feel as if my under-construction life had been duly noted. And through that imagined witnessing, somehow, a sense of repair came over me.

Something as unremarkable and unexpected as a traffic cone awakened me to new opportunities to peel back a heavy layer of unresolved tasks whose weight was suddenly evident. I called the handyman, and together we hoisted my treadmill back into the house from the garage. I bought my first new pair of running shoes since my foot size had grown in pregnancy.

I discover that Theo's 5:30 A.M. waking time allowed me to cook a wonderful meal in the morning that we could sit down to enjoy when we returned home at dinner time. I used my middle-of-the night waking times to do the writing I wished I could complete during the day. I bought the new computer whose necessity paralleled the running shoes. I got the blood test that my doctor had recommended a year earlier, and then the iron supplements that the test indicated I needed.

Spontaneously, my under-construction writing life became simpler, clearer, more streamlined. The activities that I needed in order to feel rested, friendly, inspired, and invigorated found their way into those dense days that had previously seemed impenetrable.

Though eventually I did get rid of the traffic cone, its public proclamation of a writing life under construction still resonates with me. I am grateful for the ways that a single, well-chosen symbol can bless us, galvanize us to release our burdens, and invite us into the ease that is always waiting, if we learn to allow it.

BE FIERCE

How do you honor your under-construction writing life? What symbols help you move through the places where you're stuck, scared, or struggling? Could you take one small action to set your wheels in motion?

BETTER THAN BUSY

STEPPING OUT OF THE BUSYNESS, STOPPING OUR ENDLESS PURSUIT OF GETTING SOMEWHERE ELSE, IS PERHAPS THE MOST BEAUTIFUL OFFERING WE CAN MAKE TO OUR SPIRIT. —*Tara Brach*

Mark and I were in Bend, Oregon, for the weekend. He was attending a conference, and I had tagged along to write. A major writing deadline was fast approaching, and I was delighted to have a small oasis of creative space in the midst of running a business and a household alone while solo-parenting one seven-year-old and four animals, three of whom were ailing.

As I walked to a café for breakfast with my laptop bag slung across my chest, I felt weightless. For this brief window of time, I was responsible for no one but myself. I studied the charming houses as I wandered at my own pace through a bright neighborhood that glittered with recent rain. I breathed in deeply and felt my feet land solidly upon the earth. I came upon a little hen house at the edge of a yard. Inside its open door sat a chicken placidly on her nest.

I knelt down and gazed at her. She gazed back at me. I'm not sure what moved me to start cheering her on, but I told that chicken what a wonderful job she was doing, warming her eggs. I told her what a wonderful mother she was going to be. The chicken blinked back, offering no evidence that she needed or appreciated my reassurance. But as I spoke to her, something settled in me. It became obvious that my words to the chicken were actually for myself.

Alan Cohen says, "Busyness is not a reason for not getting other things done. It is an excuse for not claiming your true priorities." Seems to me that chickens know their true priorities. And I had something to learn from this lovely lady performing her biologically imprinted task in someone's front yard.

The chicken wasn't talking to a client, folding laundry, writing lists of groceries and household chores, petting a cat, checking the time, and obsessing about the unwashed dishes while also keeping her eggs warm. She had one job to do, and she was doing it fully. It occurred to me that I, too, was doing one thing fully at that moment: praising this chicken. We were both entirely in the present, each doing a single thing together.

As I squatted on the sidewalk in our awkward communion, I remembered a walk I'd taken through the Mount Tabor hills with Mark recently. He was amused at how slow our progress was because I found it absolutely necessary to pet and have a conversation with every cat and dog we passed. I realized that no matter how rushed I am, no matter how many conflicting priorities I have, I always believe I have the time to stop and visit with an animal.

What if I could choose to believe the same thing about my writing life? I wondered. *What if I believed that I always had enough time for my writing—because there was no acceptable alternative?*

Of course, it takes a bit longer to produce a piece of writing than to pet a few cats. But our opportunity is to create the kind of singular focus we need when it is time to write, and to stem the tide of busyness that threatens to wash us out to sea.

After parting ways with the chicken, I made my way to the café where my writing ideation happened alongside some eggs Benedict that faced a very different fate from the chicken's eggs. I had temporarily removed the responsibilities of my home environment and replaced them with the happy din of breakfasting strangers. My only job was to dream onto the page. In a nest of deliciously unimportant background noise, I spent the next six hours deep in a stream of uninterrupted writing.

This entire excursion confirmed for me that the antidote to busyness is clarity. When we are busy, it's easy to lose perspective. We can miss the opportunity to appreciate what we are doing and why. We can lose focus on whether our actions are an expression of our desires. Whereas, when we set our sights on a specific goal or destination and take coherent steps to reach it, our to-do list can have an honorable place on that path.

When we passionately want the labors of our writing lives to move us through the fragile shells of our potential into greater viability, we can organize our choices in that direction: by choosing dry and sturdy shelter for our roost, weaving the right materials into our nest, and then showing up every day for the critical act of sitting—and writing.

Though we will always have much to do, we can exit the loop of overwhelm by doing one thing at a time, with our full attention. We can honor the work we are doing by taking each step to completion. With each hatchling we bring into the world, we anchor our practice of action clarified by intention. We make a case for ourselves as writers who use our time in service to what matters. And in this context, our stories about time no longer constrict and paralyze us. We know we have the time we'll need to get our work done, because we've clarified our priorities and proven ourselves reliable to them.

BE FIERCE

A busy chicken doesn't hatch an egg. And a busy writer risks fragmentation that erodes joy and momentum. How can you set yourself up for an experience that is better than busy? How will you align your actions with desire to ensure that the eggs you value most will hatch? What strategies and attitudes keep you awake to the priority of writing, such that you are less vulnerable to distraction? Come on over to fierceonthepage.com/betterthanbusy and let's compare notes!

FIND ELIZA

In my late twenties, as my boyfriend Sanford and I were leaving San Francisco to catch our flight to Oaxaca, Mexico, I grabbed a pad of sticky notes. I wrote "Find Eliza" on its uppermost square, stuck the note on my computer screen, zipped up my suitcase, and walked out the door.

Eliza was my best friend from college. We'd fallen out of touch over the years, and I was hoping that she still lived in San Francisco—and that we could rekindle our connection when I returned from Mexico. This had been on my mind for a few months, and I didn't want to forget it during our month-long trip.

By the time we had traversed Oaxaca and landed in the tiny beach community of Puerto Ángel, I had come down with Montezuma's revenge and was sicker than I'd ever been. While I spent my days sleeping in our small room and struggling to make it from the bed to the bathroom, Sanford was out visiting his friends in the community where he had lived years before I knew him, and befriending the international travelers staying at our *casa*.

By day ten, I was ready to attempt some oatmeal. I shuffled out of our room to the communal patio where Sanford was lounging in a hammock. "Hey, Sage, you're up!" he said, "You've gotta meet my new friend!" A woman stood up from the gently swinging hammock next to Sanford.

This woman was Eliza.

Within a few weeks of writing down "Find Eliza," I'd found her—not in the city where we both lived, but in a remote coastal village in Mexico. She and my boyfriend had become buddies while I'd been sleeping off the stomach event of a lifetime. And now here we all were, on a tiled patio of a *casa* where we were all spending the week.

I was overcome. Eliza was overcome. Sanford was completely confused as we gasped, embraced each other, and then laughed wildly with disbelief.

"Remember that sticky note I put on my computer before we left for our trip?" I asked Sanford.

"Of course I do," he answered.

"Well, this is Eliza. It worked. I found her!"

Finding Eliza is probably the most dramatic example of synchronicity in a lifetime full of happy accidents and goals that have been fulfilled because I have written something down. I don't know how or why it works, but when we commit an idea, a desire, or a possibility to writing, it puts the cosmic gears in motion.

A few years after my divorce, I created a rather detailed PowerPoint presentation that described the man I would partner with next. (My friends teased me mercilessly about this, but I knew from experience that writing things down is alchemical, and I was intent on calling my true love in—without overlooking any important details.)

This lovely little presentation fastidiously documented all I had learned in relationships past. The portrait I painted in words was so vivid that when a man who seemed to radiate light was sitting across the dinner table from me a few years later, I was as certain that I'd found Mr. Right as I was that I'd found Eliza. And I remain certain today.

As writers, we invent worlds. We introduce contexts, conflicts, resolutions, revolutions, and transformations that have never existed before. Through the imagery, language, characters, and narratives of our making, we inject people, places, and possibilities into our own bloodstream and that of our readers. Every word we write tilts the world just a bit in some new and unprecedented direction.

Whether you're writing a novel, a poem, an essay, or a shopping list, I invite you to marvel at the power of the word to manifest your thought, your vision, your great ache, your clear intention. Pay attention to what you write, and what comes of it. When some unexpected moment of connection leaps from the page to the hammock in your cross-continental *casa*, take note. Give thanks. Embrace the mystery. I believe this is how words become arbiters of possibility, as we steer ourselves toward greater and greater probabilities.

BE FIERCE

How do you intend to use words to steer the craft of your life in the direction you want to go next? I invite you to write down something you want on a sticky note, put it on your computer screen or bathroom mirror or car dashboard—something you look at regularly—and see what happens next. It doesn't have to be a big or complicated desire. Just something you really want, that you're not sure how to get. Come tell us what you want, or how your sticky note became your magic wand, at fierceon thepage.com/findeliza!

IT'S YOUR STORY TO TELL

In the early days of my divorce, when I was a barn burning down, I wrote words of destruction, rage, revenge. When the smoke cleared and I could see the moon, I wrote about grief—and followed it all the way back to my childhood. Story by story, I picked the bones of my past clean. I fully digested my choices, my disappointments, my hopes, and my hurts until I came to a wide-open field of acceptance.

In time, I wanted to send stories from this rooted and sure place inside me to the surface, where other divorcing parents were just starting to go under. I wanted to offer them a lifeline. I registered the name radicaldivorce.com, and I set out to create a blog that would serve as a virtual kitchen table where I could sit down with a box of tissues and a cup of tea, and welcome parents struggling to find their way forward into new incarnations of self and family.

I hired a lovely woman to help me build and design the blog. As we set out to strategically deliver my vision, I culled dozens of short essay posts and poems from a few years' worth of writing to get me started. I was fanatically focused on delivering extraordinary content to my cherished imaginary audience. So focused that I had neglected to consider one rather significant reader: my ex-husband, Pete.

● ● ●

The night before the blog's go-live date, I woke in a sweat. I was about to go public with some of the most intimate stories of my marriage, some of the most explosive pain of my life. And Pete was the antagonist in the crosshairs of my investigation. As the father of my five-year-old son, Pete would be a person of primary importance in my life for many years to come. I had no blueprint for navigating my responsibility to my truth in tandem with my responsibility to my family.

Now, Pete married a writer. And he divorced a writer. And the liabilities of such choices are obvious. He knew loosely of my Radical Divorce aspirations: that my goal was to help people cultivate the kind of child-centered, collaborative friendship that he and I had worked so hard to establish. But he was not aware of the years of personal process I had gone through to get there. He had been spared the excruciating details of my quest to forgive him, forgive myself, make peace, and rebuild my happiness from the ground up. These were the stories I intended to tell on the blog.

While I didn't feel that I needed Pete's permission, I felt I owed him a heads-up. At the end of that anguished night, I delayed the blog's launch date and arranged a meeting. This became a galvanizing moment in my writing career.

I created a manifesto of sorts in which I articulated for myself, in writing, some bylaws of personal essay and memoir writing. Here I clarified my moral position on the healing power of truth telling—no matter how ugly the facts might be. I fortified my courage for the inevitable backlash that comes with taking an unpopular public position. And I anchored my own integrity in what I intended to share and how. Then I was ready to include Pete.

● ● ●

Looking out through the Plexiglas that divided our son's indoor soccer class from our little wobbly table, I explained to Pete that, yes, Radical Divorce would celebrate our happily-ever-after blended family, in which Pete and his post- and pre-divorce wives routinely attend birthday parties together and confuse all the grandparents. But more important, it would meet parents in their most frightened and wobbly places, and invite them to explore the opportunities to make a bad situation better for their kids—and for themselves.

Yes, Pete deserved a great deal of credit for meeting me halfway, but I could not tell his story. I could only tell my own and show how the choices I made helped us arrive at a deeper trust and kindness in divorce than we ever approached in marriage. If I was going to help anyone, I explained, I was going to need to expose my most broken and hollowed-out places in order to trace an authentic trajectory to our family's current relative peace and ease.

First Pete was scared. Then defensive. "If you're the hero of your story, that makes me the villain," he countered.

"Yes, once I saw you as a villain, and that is part of the story. But then I made a choice to see you as a teacher. And this is my position. We came together and apart in ways that I needed, to go deeper in my evolution as a person. And the deeper I go, the more capable I am as Theo's mother and your co-parent. I will share ugly moments that hurt me—not to make you wrong but to explore how we worked together to make it right. You can trust that I mean you no harm."

His shoulders went down, and his voice softened. The wild eyes of our rocky years gave way to a more sure and steady vision. Pete told me he trusted me to tell our story responsibly. I thanked him for his trust. The blog went live.

• • •

The tricky thing about telling the truth is that there is no single truth. A diamond causes endless refractions, and so do the events we live through. How we dig up a moment, shape it, and polish it influences what we can see and feel at any given time. But this process is in constant flow, as we are. For me, the distance between what happened and what was experienced is best bridged in story. Through writing, I instruct myself about how to integrate who I've been and who I'm becoming.

• • •

A few months after the launch of Radical Divorce, a Facebook friend and reader of my blog introduced me to a *New York Times* columnist who was writing about divorce. I spoke to the journalist for an hour as part of a pre-interview for her column that ran a reportage-style "he said/

she said" look at why couples divorce. I thought it would be an interesting opportunity for Pete to have a voice in our story and for us to explore how our stories (each procured through independent interviews) aligned—or didn't.

As the journalist pressed me for my thesis statement about why our marriage ended, I became increasingly uncomfortable. I was giving her metaphors about the mismatch of my depths and Pete's heights, but she wanted facts.

"Remember that New Yorkers are going to be reading this article. They're going to want to understand what actually happened here," she advised, steering me toward the clincher.

The problem wasn't that I had grown too "woo-woo" since moving to the West Coast to give a clear, factual answer. Though it took me a few hours after our call to understand, the problem was that I was fundamentally opposed to giving such an answer.

Pete and I had not betrayed each other in any kind of conventional way. There had been no affair. No lies or deceit or violence. I could point to a very specific moment when I knew it was over, but this was my moment and it was hinged to a lifetime of moments that could not be summed up in one sentence. There seemed no way to say it without blame. And this was the whole point of my project—to move away from blame and instead seek the opportunities of each heartbreak and hardship.

I knew enough from a lifetime of storytelling to expect that twenty years from now, Pete and I would likely each have a sentence or two that distilled the entire experience of our relationship to a "why it ended" synopsis. Maybe we'd even use the same two sentences. But it was all still too fresh. I was still writing myself out of the hole. I could not send the arrow of a summary statement through my heart or his. Whatever I might say would not be true enough and might not even be true at all.

What I discovered after speaking to this journalist is that I was not willing to let anyone, not even *The New York Times*, have a say in how I tell my story or decide which were the pertinent moments to lift out of the whole blurry mess of years.

Mining, shaping, and polishing the story was all I had. I needed to find my way with it. I'd deliver the "how I knew it was over" thesis statement when I was good and ready. When I felt I could do so responsibly. In a way that my son could digest when he came upon it someday. In a way that my ex-husband's extended family could breathe in. In a way that I could live with, knowing that nothing we say is true for much longer than the moment when it passes through our lips or our storytelling fingers.

● ● ●

I was terrified that speaking my truth would destroy our tenuously reconstructed family, but the opposite proved to be true. Radical Divorce has brought Pete and me closer. The more I write, the more compassion I have for both of us. And the more I scrape blame clean out of the clay, the more supple and collaborative our co-construction becomes.

Writing has taught me to live with the imprecision of truth, to tend it with my words and my devotion. And to let the stories carve new passages through me as they flow back to their source, without holding on too tight to them.

I don't know if Pete has ever read the blog. I don't know if he ever will. But I write with love for his humanity and for mine. With love for our mistakes, our anguish, our broken little mending family. All of us have been stretched in new directions.

Just as they say smiling can make you happy, writing has a similar capacity to shape emotion. Committing to a fierce respect of my co-parent on the page called me back to a respect for him in everyday life that I had lost along the way. Honoring him as the father of my child and the dark angel of some of my most complicated life lessons has helped me respect the wisdom that grief and rage bring.

Staying with the story, as it turns out, is very much like staying with the co-parent. The marriage ends, but the family continues. Word by word, we find our way.

NOTE: This essay first appeared in *The Truth of Memoir* by Kerry Cohen.

ASK WELL AND YE SHALL RECEIVE

In one of my graduate school poetry workshops, ten students got into a heated debate about one student's poem. (The rule in workshops is that the poet doesn't explain herself. Instead she listens to her peers to discover how they are experiencing the poem.) As is often the case, every person in the room had their own interpretation of what was happening in this particular poem, the two most memorable being that the speaker was either having sex or that she was vomiting.

Such are the liabilities of subjectivity in art. We can count on the reader to take in our work through the lens of himself and to find, at best, some part of what we are offering mingled with what he is seeking.

After this workshop, I went home and wrote a poem depicting each of these ten students critiquing a poem. In my poem, each person delivered the same classic feedback they reliably gave about every poem we workshopped together, based on their particular preferences, aesthetic, and cosmology about poetry. Through this amusing exercise, I taught myself that the feedback we get is biased, and our job as poets and writers is to learn how to listen for those biases and interpret the critiques we get in the way that best serves our work.

Asking for help—and making good use of it—is an art unto itself in the writing life. I invite you to experiment with a range of input and focus on discerning what works best for you. For example, your best friend might be the perfect person to go rock climbing with, but he might not know how to respond to a personal essay. Your writing group might be the exact right fit. But you won't know until you pay close attention to the feedback you get and how you use it.

I'd like to offer some guidelines to help you invite the best possible support for your work and your process.

DON'T RUSH TO SHARE YOUR WRITING; WAIT UNTIL YOU FEEL READY. One of the most common mistakes I see writers make is sharing their work and inviting critical commentary before they are truly ready to accept it. Feedback can be particularly painful and confusing when you're not yet grounded in your writing practice, your sense of direction for your work, and your sense of your writer-self. I wrote poems for a decade before sharing my writing. Even then, it was difficult to talk with others about them. It took probably another decade of engaging in critique before I started to get a true sense of how to best use feedback. You needn't hurry to get your work in front of people.

PAY ATTENTION TO THE FEEDBACK AND SUPPORT THAT YOU FIND MOST USEFUL. To elaborate on the above point: Let's say you're in a writing group, and you're getting conflicting feedback from various members. Your job is to recognize whose suggestions work best for you. As I did in my writing workshop, pay attention to the tendencies of your readers and the patterns of their feedback. If you wrote about sex and a reader interpreted it to mean vomiting, it could be that your piece needs work. Or it could be that this reader is simply inclined to land on intestinal distress when attempting to decipher a piece.

Of all the contrasting feedback, what feels right? Who in the group seems to understand what you're trying to accomplish? When you experiment with adapting feedback in your work, what is most useful? When you log these insights over time, you will start to understand who is part of your brain trust, and you can focus on how their insights help you grow.

IF IT SOUNDS WRONG OR FEELS WRONG, OR SIMPLY DOESN'T WORK FOR YOU, IT PROBABLY *IS* WRONG. It's easy to get tangled up in advice that isn't suited for who you are and what you're trying to accomplish. No matter who the expert is, or how smart his or her suggestions sound, if the help you're receiving isn't working for you, move on.

BE SPECIFIC WHEN YOU ASK FOR HELP OR FEEDBACK. Maybe your mom tells you everything you write is great and your wife points out only the flaws. Or maybe everyone in your writing group is being too nice and you'd like them to be more critical. Or vice versa. Try telling your readers, editors, or collaborators exactly what you want from them. "Mom, I'd like you to point out three examples of scenes that could be better developed," or "Writing group, it would be great if we could talk about the strengths of this piece of writing." If you find that the people or groups you turn to for feedback are not able to provide the kind of support you'd prefer, keep exploring other readers or groups until you find the right fit.

IT'S OKAY NOT TO KNOW. Maybe you don't know what you want or need from your writing community or teachers. No problem. We all start in the place of not knowing. Just pay attention to what moves you forward and what holds you back. When someone challenges an image you've crafted, does it compel you to write it better, or does it make you want to hide under your desk for a week? There is no right or wrong way in the writing life—there is only your way. And your job as a writer is to find your unique path and cultivate it to the best of your ability. You will likely go through 'different phases where your needs change. If you're listening for what works, not knowing can lead you to your most fertile insights and truths.

BE FIERCE

Who can you count on for feedback that helps move your work ahead? How could you refine your requests to get the same kind of support from everyone in your writing life? Are there people in your inner-feedback circle who don't belong there? How do you know when you're ready to share a piece?

FREEDOM'S JUST ANOTHER WORD FOR NOTHING LEFT TO CHOOSE

It's great to have options in our writing lives. And yet, an unexpected series of events led me to believe that unlimited options may not be as beneficial as they first appear.

The year I became a single mom, my financial and logistical options were dramatically limited, for what appeared to be the worse. While I once had the option to leave the house to attend readings, lecture, teach, and have fun with friends, those choices now evaporated. The money I once spent on books, workshops, travel, and dog food instead funded my new, primary relationship with a divorce lawyer. Perhaps most painfully, I canceled four online classes I had planned to teach after realizing that I did not have the emotional or intellectual reserves to effectively facilitate.

Bummer, right? Yes, but that's not the whole story.

Something rather incredible happened in this interpersonal limbo: I gained spaciousness. I was no longer burdened with the decisions of which events to attend, or which of my many dear friends I would support as they read and performed publicly nearly every night of the week. Nor was I burdened with the decisions of how to invest in my writing life—or where to designate funds for anything, for that matter, as I didn't have funds to designate. Giving service to my literary community was not an option. The fact was that I couldn't do any of it at that time. Period.

Now, I'm not advocating being broke and stranded at home as a productivity practice or a way of life. But I do want you to know that in my own life, which has been quite abundant with options and opportunities since I started working for myself in 1997, such deprivations facilitated a rather surprising liberation. In the absence of choice, peace started filling the open spaces.

One afternoon, as the sun made a brief appearance between avalanches of hail, Theo stood in a beam of light, marveling at the floating specks of dust that shone like diamonds all around us. This was the new wealth of our life together: diamonds of dust, necklaces of ABCs. No rush to do much of anything in a life that was once overflowing with hour upon hour upon hour of scheduled tasks and meetings, stacked like the precarious towers Theo built from blocks. We giggled as he smashed those towers down, and he told me that his voice sounded better than mine as we sang "The Farmer in the Dell," his longtime favorite.

During my divorce year, I spent evenings cooking for Theo, writing, making my home beautiful, and dining in with friends who showed up with meals, stories, and love. I dug out from the tornado of clothes, paper, and toys that seemed to have spontaneously birthed alongside my son. I wrote a business plan for my writing life, simmered five or so new book ideas on the back burner of my consciousness, and did what I needed to do to get the dogs walked and the mortgage paid. Slowly my grief and rage transmuted to peace and forgiveness. My life and heart became full in completely different ways than they had been just a short time ago, when I was married.

And despite the fact that I don't sing as well as my two-year-old did then, I came up with my own version of Janis Joplin's "Me and Bobby McGee." It goes like this:

> Windshield wipers slapping time
> I was holding Theo's hand in mine
> and we sang every song that toddler knew
> 'Cause freedom's just another word for nothing left to choose
> And nothing don't mean nothing, honey, if it ain't free … yeah

BE FIERCE

Is something you view as a major obstacle in your writing life actually liberating you from a less true path, from commitments that don't serve you, or from something you aren't actually called to do but feel you should be doing? If there is an area in your writing life where you have fewer options than you would like, could you see it as an opportunity instead of a limitation? How might the challenges you're facing free up time, energy, or space so you can do more of what's important to you—or less of what isn't? What seems to be lacking in your writing life might actually be a gain if you simply look at it through the diamonds of dust pouring over you at this very minute.

WRITE YOUR MANIFESTO

When you are clear about who you are as a writer—meaning you know what you write and for whom—you can create more coherently and productively. The tricky part is that people evolve. Life stages and life events will inevitably shape you. The words you read and write will transform you. And the company you keep will mirror you in ways that influence your path.

For many years, I thought my creative writing and marketing writing were two entirely separate enterprises—because they were. Likewise, I thought my lifelong pursuit of personal evolution had nothing to do with my writing life, even though writing was always my primary transportation toward healing, growth, clarity, and authenticity.

Now, thirty-plus years after I started writing poems in my pink suburban bedroom, twenty-plus years after I started writing professionally, and forty-five years after my journey on Earth began, my sense of myself as a writer and a human has coalesced. I can see and appreciate how writing poems makes me a more strategic business communicator. I can see how the virtues I cherish in friendship translate to the commitments I make to my students. And I understand that I write primarily to create transportation through transformation.

The going wisdom for writers is to specialize. As useful as it may be for you to home in on a specialty or two, this kind of focus runs the risk of missing the big picture of who you are as person and a writer. Is your writing identity expansive enough to include all of you? Is there some dimension of your writing life that you don't think is "legitimate"? Could your writing identity use a bit of updating?

I have come to accept that the writing life is expansive enough to hold my many refractions, and that these add up to the whole of what I have to give. Today, I see my writing and teaching identity like this:

> Stories are the currency of life and business. The stories we tell have the power to shape thought, feelings, choices, and lives. I use the written word to help people fulfill goals, make discoveries, and expand their sense of possibility, so that we all can write better and live better.

I call this my writing manifesto. It's a distillation of what I believe about writing, what I value, and why I write. Informed by a lifetime of experience, my manifesto is the North Star of my writing practice. I have a printed copy hanging over my desk so I can call myself back when I'm lost, scared, or need to remind myself why the work I'm doing matters to me.

My manifesto will evolve as I do, challenging me to be bolder and braver in writing the words I am here to contribute. So can yours.

BE FIERCE

Write your manifesto by summing up your writing life in three sentences:

1. What do you believe about writing in general?
2. What do you believe about your writing in particular?
3. What do you intend to accomplish in your writing life?

Don't think about this too long—write what first comes to mind. Know that you can always update your manifesto as you understand more about your work and yourself.

Now post your writing manifesto prominently in a place where you can refer to it often. Then share it with our fierce writing community at fierceonthepage.com/manifesto. Declaring who you are as a writer is alchemical. Knowing where you're headed and what makes your engine go can make you unstoppable.

LOVE THY LIST

I found out this week, by chance, that my longtime veterinarian sold his practice and is moving out of town. Without even so much as a farewell form letter, he is simply closing up shop and disappearing into the Oregon fog. With a business of my own, built on decades of investment in good relationships, this news astounded me. I imagined pet owners all over Portland getting that "he's just not that into you" slap in the face when they called to make an appointment with their trusted veterinarian and were told that he has moved on without bothering to mention it.

This veterinary saga brings me to my latest technology saga: my database. I've been self-employed for eighteen years, and in all that time, I have been faithfully entering the names and contact info of my friends, family, clients, colleagues, literary community members, media lists, and folks who specifically sign up to hear from me. I started sending holiday cards to all five hundred. Then, as the list grew over time, I sent valentines to all one thousand—then two thousand. And, of course, I send handwritten notes whenever possible, because they are my favorite way to connect.

One summer during my college years, I temped as a receptionist for an organization that provided in-home nurse aides. I had two people on hold: an elder person with incontinence issues who wanted to talk to a nurse, and a contractor who was renovating the home of one of the employees in the office. Somehow, those two hold lines mistakenly merged, and the contractor ended up fielding the incontinence call, much to his dismay.

I discovered recently that something similar had happened to my database. A streamlined list of about three thousand names somehow started leaping their fences and mingling with information from other entries, replicating whatever struck their fancy, to the tune of sixteen thousand spontaneously generated and mangled records. I saw it as a database cancer of sorts.

I spent many days cleaning up the mess, and it was quite frustrating. But as with all mistakes and mishaps, a very interesting gift surfaced: a journey of gratitude through my past. As I sorted through thousands of names and parsed the meaningful from the nonsense, I savored the rare opportunity to reacquaint myself with people from my past—people I like very much but haven't thought of for years. Just seeing how many humans have touched my life enough for me to add them to the database made me feel connected in ways that I don't often experience when I'm alone in my house, at my desk, with cats in my lap and the occasional conference call to connect me to the outside world.

And then, something even stranger than database-record mating started happening. A good friend and colleague from three cities ago called from his latest city to offer me a job. Another three friend-colleagues whom I hadn't seen or spoken to in nearly a decade sent letters of introduction to potential new clients. I was invited to read as part of a poetry series. One of my best friends from college—with whom I'd last spoke in 1996—called to catch up. Work was pouring in, and friends were showing up to walk my dogs, feed me, or play with Theo.

Just engaging with and *appreciating* my list literally seemed to magnetize me to what I wanted and needed most.

Which brings me back to my shock and confusion about the veterinarian. He had this incredible list of people who depended on him, who adored him, and he didn't complete the circuit to say, *Goodbye* or *Thank you*, or *I'm sorry your dog will die of that disease, but I do hope the medication makes him comfortable.* He didn't love his list. And I imagine that is now costing him a foundation he spent his entire career building.

I believe every writer needs to honor, cherish, and tend his or her list of friends, colleagues, teachers, publishers, family, media, readers, students, and more.

The writing life is solitary in some ways, but like any endeavor that involves other people—colleagues, readers, publishers, editors—a significant source of potential happiness or unhappiness lies in the relationships you cultivate. Keep in touch with these people who matter to you. Make it clear that you value their interests, friendship, expertise, or whatever else. But even more important than telling *them* what you appreciate, tell *yourself* what you appreciate about the community you are cultivating as you hold those names and faces in your mind.

When you love your list, it will love you back. Try it, and you'll see what I mean.

BE FIERCE

How will you honor and cultivate the relationships you already have? How will you thank the people in your literary community for the value you are co-creating with them? What would they want to know about your work and your writing life? Who do you want to know better? Who do you intend to add to your database this year? How can you love your list a little every day? Let's compare our best strategies at fierceonthepage.com/lovethylist.

WRITE THE ACKNOWLEDGMENTS FIRST

When Theo was diagnosed with his first two cavities at age six, the dentist scheduled a test-run appointment so we could walk through each step of the cavity-filling process and Theo would know exactly what to expect when he showed up for his actual appointment. My kiddo tested the laughing gas, felt the drill gently moving on his palm, witnessed a demonstration of how the filling sealant is applied and how quickly it dries, and reviewed the selection of videos he could choose from on the day of the procedure.

My son left his test-run appointment having demystified the whole realm of dental cavity intervention. He was hugely reassured that there would be no surprises he couldn't handle. This set us up for a low-drama, high-satisfaction dental event.

As Theo was being kindly guided through his practice run, I considered how much more stability, ease, and trust we could all generate for ourselves if we took the time to prepare a mental picture of where we are headed and establish how we want our needs to be met when we arrive. A self-soothing visualization of sorts.

The Law of Attraction suggests that we inhabit our desired future emotionally and thus predispose our nervous system for the joys and the gratitude that await us. By living *as if* that desired reality has already happened, we become more receptive to it.

As a writer, you can do this by compiling the acknowledgments for your book before you even start writing it. Or, as a more open-ended possibility, you could draft a thank-you letter to the Universe for the future event, success, or state of being you expect to be grateful for. Or, even more specifically, you could write (but not send) advance thanks to the editors, agents, publications, or collaborators to whom you intend to be grateful to at some point in the future.

I've experimented with all of these strategies enough to believe that they are worth your time and attention. Of course, the cause and effect of such efforts are always debatable. But for me, the practice of gratitude is so satisfying that it has become an end in itself. If and when it attracts what I am calling in, all the better.

Here's what happened for me. I committed to a deep gratitude practice in the three areas of my life where I wanted to manifest very specific, very big goals: writing, relationship, and motherhood. In each instance, it took between four and five years of intention, gratitude, and strategic action to move myself from vision into reality.

I wrote ridiculously specific thank-you letters to the Universe for what I intended to come my way. I detailed the many different dimensions by which my needs would be met and desires fulfilled. I didn't just focus on my gratitude for what I expected to manifest, but how I imagined I would *feel* once my life was full of what I wanted. I even started a one-way correspondence with my imagined beloved. I wrote him e-mails to an in-box I invented for him, discussing the things I wished to one day discuss with him after he appeared.

The more I wrote, the clearer I became about my vision for the future and my passion for my goals. This practice helped me recognize and engage with the opportunities that led to my first two books. I imprinted the joys of motherhood I expected to live and was incredibly fortunate to then experience them. This practice also lifted me out of the rubble of divorce into an exalted vision informed by all I had learned in my marriage. Over time, my ideal partner became more recognizable in my mind, as I cultivated a paradigm for deep happiness and mutuality that I had yet to manifest. I felt his arms around me years before I saw him walking down the street toward me for the first time.

Now let's consider how this could work for you.

Imagine that you have a completed manuscript under your belt. It could be the final version of the one you're working on right now. Or it could be the one you've always dreamed of. Now answer these questions to craft your acknowledgments.

- Which teachers and mentors from your early years helped your formative writer-self take root?
- Which publications accepted the poems, chapters, or excerpts that appear in this volume? Imagine this as specifically as you can.
- Which colleagues or members of your writing group grappled with you in the mosh pit of scene, image, and character? (Let's say you don't even have a writing group yet. Who will be in the one that you will create or join?)
- Which agent and/or editors believed in you, guided you, or challenged you to bring your best work forward?
- How does it feel to have such a multifaceted tribe supporting your work, believing in you and contributing to your success?
- How does each person or publication specifically contribute to the evolution or end-goal of your work?
- What does your future writer-self dress like, talk like, and eat for breakfast? Who does this future you call for guidance or support? What are the rhythms of your future self's days?

I've watched master gardeners dedicate years to a future harvest: fertilizing the soil and making sure it has the proper PH and nutrients for what they intend to plant in it. We have similar opportunities and responsibilities as writers. The more palpable our gratitude, the more receptive we become to what we are calling in.

BE FIERCE

Living *as if*, writing *as if*, plunks us directly into the future state we intend to inhabit. Once we've visited, we have a far greater likelihood of finding our way to it in real time.

A BUG'S LIFE, A WRITER'S LIFE

If you haven't seen the movie *A Bug's Life* recently, here's a quick overview of a key plot point: A misfit ant faces an impassible canyon as he attempts to leave the only life he has ever known on a quest to save his colony. As he contemplates his next move at the cliff's edge, three young ants stand behind him. One ant projects that this crusader will give up in an hour, while another believes he will die. A third perky little preschooler says she thinks he'll succeed.

Sound familiar?

Much like this strapping, deluded little insect, each of us stands at our own version of this impasse from time to time. With a chorus of voices at our backs chattering all kinds of nonsense, we sway in the vertigo of "How do I get from here to there?"

Forgive me for giving the moment away: This inventive ant climbs up a dandelion stem, plucks a seed from its puff of possibility, and then drifts into the canyon, using the seed as a parachute. Obstacle transformed with just a bit of Pixar animation magic.

Writers have a unique opportunity to write ourselves off such cliffs and into fresh terrain where the circus bugs might save us. In fact, lately I have come to respect writing as an unsung form of transportation. Where can it take you that you don't yet know how to go?

In recent years, as I transitioned from family life to single motherhood, most of my ideas about myself crumbled, leaving me with no bridge between the person I thought I was and the person now standing at the cliff's edge. One thing was clear: I had to leave my current life to save the one I would have in the future. Writing has always been the little seedpod that holds the treasure of what can be discovered. With it,

I took the leap into the unknown and then documented it with curiosity on the way down.

As my life unwound from its previous interpretation, I turned my words into the wind and for the first time in my life let myself be carried far beyond anyplace I had traveled, far beyond anyplace I wanted to go or knew how to go. Sure, some of the landings have been comedic face plants (or "face flowers," as my son once called them) into boulders. But I had a self and a family to save. I was going to discover the words to right myself and find my way. You will, too.

When you're at an impasse of transition, and your next steps are unclear, follow the words. Trust the words. Trust the cliffs, the canyons, the face flowers. Trust your disorientation and your sense of direction. Trust what you find and don't find. The shadow gives shape to light. These are your stories. The dance of interdependence is a hum of words.

BE FIERCE

What do you want to accomplish in your writing or in your life, but aren't sure how to achieve? What crossing can your writing help you make? What leaps can it help you take? Write about this desire for ten minutes, pretending you know how to proceed. What would you advise yourself to try next? Where might your writing teach you to go?

LEAD WHAT YOU WANT TO LEARN

IF YOU'RE IN SECOND GRADE, THE FOURTH GRADER IS AN EXPERT.
—Danny Iny

When I moved to Portland, Oregon, and wanted to plug into the literary scene, I decided to host a reading series. I didn't know a single writer in town. I didn't know any local literary venues. What I did know was that I'd be accountable to my desire to delve deep into my new literary landscape if I put myself in charge of an event that required me to do so.

My good friend Nicole was also new to town and had a cozy gathering space in the basement of her fabulous Bold-Sky Cafe. We quickly established a thriving micro-mecca that celebrated local poets. I didn't know how to run a reading series when I started. But I knew how to love people and poems, and I figured out the rest as I went. As I immersed myself in my new literary community, I was awed at the talent, the generosity, and the integrity of the writers I had the privilege to showcase for the next five years.

Through this experience, I learned how taking a leadership role increases the risk, the commitment, and the reward. Which is why I quickly moved on to teaching, lecturing, and authoring. I was not called to these choices because I felt certain of my expertise. I was called to challenge myself to learn more about what mattered to me and to then share what I love with other people who wanted to join me in conversation.

We are called to teach because we are called to study. Whatever you have devoted yourself to learn in your writing life, you also have the opportunity to lead.

Teaching what you are dedicated to discovering is a powerful way to go deeper into your craft and to anchor what you know while making a meaningful contribution to your community.

The secret is that you don't need to be the world's leading expert on your chosen topic to teach a course in it. You just need to know enough about it to be useful to people who are not as far along on the learning curve. For example, I taught creative writing to college students while I was in graduate school studying creative writing. We were all students; I just had a little more practice and training than the students in my class, enough to provide meaningful facilitation of their process. These days, I teach a poetry elective in my son's elementary school, and decades later I am still discovering, alongside my students, the possibilities a poem can hold.

I've had various students over the years discredit the teaching they've done or the recognition they've earned because they didn't consider the forum they were leading to be impressive enough. I hope you won't do that—because if you are leading, you are learning. If you are showing other people the way, you are finding your own way.

There will always be people who know more or less than you. Your job as a writer is not to judge where you are on that continuum. Your job is to show up and learn from the people who have something to teach you, to become a lifelong student of your craft, and along the way to share your knowledge and enthusiasm with people who are interested in receiving it. This keeps the virtuous circle of the writing life moving everyone forward. From tenured academic positions to workshops you've organized and publicized yourself, there are a variety of forums where you could bring people together to learn what's possible in your craft. You can choose the ones that suit your experience and temperament.

As you articulate and systematize your passion and knowledge into an offering you can share with others, you teach yourself to become the expert of the realm you love to inhabit. As you increase your risk and commitment, you grow into the writer you were meant to be.

RIDE THE WAVE OF FEAR

I'VE BEEN ABSOLUTELY TERRIFIED EVERY MOMENT OF MY LIFE, AND I'VE NEVER LET IT KEEP ME FROM DOING A SINGLE THING THAT I WANTED TO DO. —*Georgia O'Keeffe*

When Theo was a toddler and I set a limit he didn't like, he told me that he was going to put me in jail. This logic intrigued me, because I see adults putting themselves in jail all the time. We do so because we are afraid, or because imprisonment seems safer than taking a real risk and failing. But if we know that we have jail to fall back on, why not experiment with freedom and see what possibilities might be waiting for us on the other side of the bars?

The writing life presents endless opportunities to meet fear. Facing the blank page, sending work out for publication, and presenting it to an audience can all be triggers. Fear is neither good nor bad—it's simply an emotional weather vane that lets us know where we are meeting or anticipating challenge.

Fear becomes a problem when we do (or don't do) something to avoid feeling it. And this is what too many of us are in the habit of doing. For example, if we let the fear of rejection prevent us from pitching or querying or submitting, we are ensuring that we'll never realize our aspirations. Even worse, we are reinforcing fear's position as captain of our craft. However, when we consciously work *with* fear, we can harness this energy source in ways that support our writing goals and enhance our writing experience. Here are ten ways to do it.

1. IDENTIFY THE WARNING SIGNS OF FEAR.

It's easy to recognize fear when we are about to throw up or pass out or run screaming out of a building. But fear has many subtler faces that can be hard to discern. If you are overperforming, underperforming, or avoiding performing at all, chances are good that fear is in play.

For example, did you ever consider that the piece of writing you just can't get right—and therefore you endlessly revise—is a reflection of your fear? That the important project you can't find time to start is likely being thwarted by fear? Even your turbocharged accomplishment mode could be driven by fear. When you find fear at the root of a challenging habit or behavior, you are fortunate—because with awareness, you have choices.

2. HONOR YOUR INNER CRITIC—BUT DON'T PUT IT IN CHARGE.

We all have negative thoughts that creep in when we are afraid. Our job is to make sure they don't short-circuit us. I often reference a movie scene when I'm working with my own inner critic. In *A Beautiful Mind*, when someone from the Nobel Prize committee asks schizophrenic mathematician John Nash how he silenced the voices that threatened to interfere with his work and his life, Nash replies something to the effect of, "I didn't. They're talking to me right now. I have simply made a choice to stop engaging with what they're saying."

Every writer has the opportunity to handle fear in this way: to learn to live with the negative stories that get airtime in our minds without letting them limit what we know we must do. Chances are good that your inner critic is trying to protect you from potential pain. Once it sees that you're going to be just fine, it will likely let up, and eventually shut up for good.

3. FOCUS ON PROCESS INSTEAD OF RESULTS.

Fear tends to be focused on projected outcomes—which we cannot control. So why not use fear as a signal to turn your attention to your process instead? What we do have influence over is the intention, commitment, and labor of love that goes into our writing. When you give your attention to following through on a goal, taking steps to improve your craft, researching places to submit, or reading a book on marketing, you are creating forward motion that makes it harder for fear to hold you back.

4. PUT PERFECTIONISM IN ITS PLACE.

Many of us have this idea that we're meant to be perfect writers, and I'm not sure where that notion comes from. We don't expect our fingerprints to be perfect. They are what they are—unique patterns that exclusively represent you—not good or bad or better or worse than anyone else's. What if we looked at our writing in the same way?

I propose that your job as a writer is to get acquainted with the writing pattern that is uniquely yours and become more proficient at expressing it. Your process doesn't have an endpoint, and you will never arrive at "perfect." So why not give up the chase and just enjoy the resonance and beauty of what you are capable of right now? Rather than "perfect" as an end goal, try setting your sights on "finished." Take it as far as you know how to go, and then consider it complete.

5. LET EASE BE YOUR COMPASS.

If you approach your writing life from a place of fear, you will likely expect that being a writer is *really hard*. Fear gets us all knotted up such that we have to work twice as hard at writing, publishing, promoting, and presenting just to overcome our resistance.

You may be so afraid of failing that you work three times harder than the average bear to prove to yourself and the world that you are successful. Such an attitude lands you shoulder to boulder, on an eternal, uphill climb. This gets tiring fast.

I spent most of my adult life trying to accomplish as much as possible in every moment. These days, I'm experimenting with doing less and trusting more. Sometimes just being still is all the writing life requires.

Sometimes we gain more when we simply allow room for growth and stop trying so hard.

6. ACKNOWLEDGE YOUR BAD HABITS, BUT DON'T INDULGE THEM.

Do you catch yourself doing just about anything to avoid a writing project that matters to you? Or, conversely, do you tend to write thirty or more drafts of one piece, unable to decide when it is finished? Try setting and enforcing some performance standards.

If you find yourself scrubbing the toilet with a toothbrush rather than starting that piece of writing you anticipate will be difficult, give yourself a time limit: ten minutes with the toothbrush and then ten minutes at your desk. Whatever happens, happens, and then you are excused. The point is to give yourself the escape valve (otherwise, you will rebel), but then make sure you actually follow through with your goal.

Similarly, the next time you catch yourself about to revise that piece yet again, try setting a cutoff limit: three drafts, total, and then you will declare the piece finished.

Like any practice, the more you implement whatever standards you set, the more reliable you will become. Experiment with various ways to accept and move through your resistance. Don't forget to be friendly to the resistance. It just wants to keep you safe. Bit by bit, you'll earn its trust.

7. DO WHAT SCARES YOU BECAUSE IT SCARES YOU.

What do you fear most in your writing life? Take a moment to evaluate if it will truly do you serious harm. If the answer is no, then I invite you to make a point of doing the very thing that scares you—as much as you can—until you exhaust fear's charge around it. I'm not suggesting that this process will be fast or easy, though that's possible. But I do know that the more ambitious you are in tackling a significant challenge, the greater your self-confidence will be on the other side.

In my own writing life, public speaking has been the numero uno fear to conquer. This first came to my attention in second grade, when I skipped callbacks for the role of Gretl in *The Sound of Music* because I was terrified that I might actually be cast. I've been working with this fear ever since.

How did I overcome it? By singing and dancing and acting in every play, performance, and band that would have me. And in the past twenty years, by reading and speaking publicly at every opportunity. Flawed and committed, I've stayed with it and I've gotten better. I've had major humiliations and significant successes. I've learned how to prepare and that I can trust myself along the way. It took a long time, but I mastered my fear of public speaking simply by relentlessly doing it.

8. KEEP YOUR EYES ON THE PRIZE.

If you have something more interesting to focus on than fear, it's far less likely that fear will hog the spotlight of your attention. One way to hold your focus elsewhere is to clearly articulate for yourself why you're working on a particular piece of writing, what motivates you to stay with it, and what the imagined end result will be.

For example, if you know that the article you're writing about cultivating organic community gardens is going to teach you about something that's both a core value and an expression of your platform, you have an intrinsic reward that's worth writing for. If you understand that meeting a deadline and a word count while earning a paycheck is going to bring you one step closer to being a professional writer, that can keep you focused on crossing those finish lines.

9. REVISE YOUR WORST-CASE SCENARIO.

Fear exists to keep us safe. If you are feeling fear, you are likely perceiving danger. The harder you try to silence the fear, the louder it will get to try to protect you. Therefore, I propose that you lean into fear and really listen to what it wants you to know. For example, consider an inquiry process like this.

YOU: Why am I unable to finish this story?

FEAR: Because if you call it "finished," then you might find out it's bad. If you never finish it, then you never have to send it out, and you'll never know. You'll be safer that way.

YOU: What's wrong with finding out it's bad?

FEAR: Then you would be a terrible writer.

YOU: According to whom?

FEAR: The people who read it. The publications that reject it.

YOU: What if I believe, instead, that I can only do my best, and commit to learning how to improve as I go? If I keep trying and keep getting better, would I be a terrible writer then?

FEAR: Well, I guess not.

YOU: In fact, wouldn't finishing something and getting feedback about it likely help me improve so that I might still, someday, be a writer I can admire?

FEAR: (Skulking) Yes.

YOU: Thanks, fear, for helping me understand why I was afraid to finish this piece. Let's work together to polish it so I can start the next one.

10. SET YOUR FEAR OF FEAR FREE.

In short, fear is not the problem—*fearing* fear is where we run into trouble. When we exit this loop, we'll be in a better place to see clearly, aspire meaningfully, and stop tripping over our own self-defeating feet.

I'm not saying that when we release fear's vise grip, all of our goals are realized and our dreams come true. However, it has been my experience that we have far more room to breathe, experiment, and evolve when we're not squeezed into those small, invented stories that have been dictated to us by fear.

Your life and your writing are both precious resources. Don't waste a drop of either. Put fear in charge of helping you see where you're ready to grow, and be curious about how to move from fear to trust. When you walk through fear's doorway, you have a chance to step into your greatest potential.

NOTE: This essay first appeared in the September 2011 issue of *Writer's Digest* magazine.

FIND YOUR FORM

LOOK FOR THE SILVER LINING. THAT'S THE BEST WAY TO FIND IT.
—Heather Strang and The Joy Team (thejoyteam.org)

In 2007, while waiting in a long line at a writing conference, I struck up a conversation with a lovely young journalist named Heather who wanted to expand her repertoire with creative writing. It seemed to me that this woman had enough drive, passion, and love of her craft to engage deeply in a weekend of learning and to leverage the input to accelerate her writing life.

A year later, I was thrilled to learn that my friend had published her first book of poems. Soon thereafter, I lost the thread of her life and career as I plunged into an abyss of new motherhood, exhaustion, and bliss.

Fast forward to 2015, when billboards from The Joy Team started popping up all over Portland. The billboards featured memorable inspirational quotes from Heather, including the one that starts this chapter. Each time a beam of her optimism reached me from on high, I delighted in the fact that Heather seemed to have landed in an exquisite cross section of encouragement and authority. I looked her up online and marveled at how her career had taken her from journalism to poetry to fiction to her latest form—the billboard.

The billboard! What an interesting literary space.

Each time I drive by Heather's exalted couplet hanging high and bright over the city like a temporary moon, I appreciate all the possibilities we have for giving voice to what we want to share. I also make note of the alchemy of converging and collaborating around a shared value or purpose—just as Heather and The Joy Team had conspired to change the advertising paradigm from selling us stuff to selling us a new perspective.

As I sit in bumper-to-bumper traffic on one of the city's main arteries and search for the silver lining in the fender of the motionless car ahead of me, I agree with Heather: Looking for the silver lining is the best way to find it. And seeking the form that embodies what we have to say is the best way to find that, too. No matter what we believe we're here to write, many of us stumble into surprising new expressions that elevate and inform our practice.

I don't know how the steps on Heather's path led her to the work she's doing today, but I do know that the practice of writing is much like the practice of parenting.

Every day, week, and year, our writing requires something different from us. And if we want it to thrive, we must frequently improvise to find fresh ways to meet those needs.

I was absolutely and unilaterally obsessed with poems—and poems only—until my early thirties. Then I started blogging and discovered that I was equally compelled by the personal essay. This led to how-to articles, nonfiction books, and, most recently, short stories. In parallel, I've been writing marketing and advertising copy for businesses for two decades. All of this mingled, cross-genre work keeps me fresh, curious, awake, and wildly engaged in solving the writing problem at hand— whether it's a B2B e-mail campaign or a haiku.

Because my work is a kaleidoscope of forms, I seek examples of other writers who not only cross genres but leapfrog, expand, or reinvent forms. David Whyte brings poetry to business. Jacqueline Suskin writes on-demand poems on her typewriter in trade for donations at farmers markets (and this is how she came to save a forest with a poem). Andrea Scher made a wish tree in front of her house and encouraged the entire neighborhood to write and hang their private wishes on small manila gift tags from its branches.

What we write, the craft in which we send it, and with whom we share it (and collaborate) matters. Finding your form may be as fluid as deciding on a given day if you'll take the kayak, the sailboat, or the jet skis.

Of course, specializing in a particular genre, form, or approach is fabulous, and most experts advise doing so. But I think things get really interesting when we stretch into areas we've never yearned to master, where it never even occurred to us that we could share a message, and see what wants to be said there.

The more we stretch, the more flexible we become. The more we seek the opportunity to put unexpected possibilities forward, the more surprising, authentic, and panoramic we become to ourselves and our readers.

BE FIERCE

What do you have to say, and where does it belong? On a billboard, a letterpress card, a tattoo on your bicep, a note on a napkin? What can writing a poem teach you about your novel, your Ph.D. dissertation, or your personal essay? What would crafting a pivotal conversation between two key characters in a series of tweets reveal—or hide? How could you involve a writing friend, your neighborhood, or your city in the exploration? See how far you can stretch your idea of form for your writing, and then note where it leads you. You never know where you'll find the silver lining until you start looking.

LISTEN TO YOUR MOTHER

I received a thank-you note today from a friend who claimed she was nervous about sending me the note because she considers me the queen of the thank-you note. As I held her card and considered this, I wondered if any title in the world (other than "Mommy") could make me happier.

I love the thank-you note. Taking the time to write down what I appreciate about another person, to simmer in that gratitude word by word, and then send it off in a pretty little envelope to arrive into that person's hands just makes me feel good.

I have my mother to thank for this discipline that has become a bedrock of my being. She insisted not only that I be grateful in writing but that I be memorable, creative, and original. The crucible of our collaboration began when I was thirteen, sitting at the kitchen table and drowning in a sea of bat mitzvah thank-you notes, hand cramped and mind exhausted. (How many different ways can you say "Thanks for your generosity," to a friend of your grandparents who you don't actually know?) If each card didn't specifically state what I appreciated about the gift and why I was glad the recipient had come to my bat mitzvah, I had to start again.

Given what I went through—two laborious weeks of writing, debating, rewriting—it surprises me that today, at the age my mother was when we labored together in my first gratitude marathon, I am a disciple of the thank-you note, humbly in service to a small gesture through which I cherish my friends, family, clients, and community.

How did it happen? I'm not sure.

The girl I was at that kitchen table could only see the burden of responsibility. And yet, the work that girl did, card after card after card, became a kind of transportation toward the woman she would become.

Now, on most days, I put a thank-you note in the mail using special letterpress cards I designed and printed for this purpose. The more cards I send, the more people I think of to thank.

For example, I hired Brant to build an arbor around my front door. I drew it exactly as I wanted, and he realized my vision perfectly. Marveling at how the arbor's beauty uplifted me every time I crossed my threshold, I called Brant a few weeks after the arbor went up (because I didn't have his mailing address). He answered the phone defensively.

"What can I do for you?" he asked, his voice terse and distant.

"You can say, 'You're welcome,'" I responded.

"I don't understand," Brant shot back.

"I am calling to say, 'Thank you.'"

Silence.

"What do you mean?" he asked.

"I love my arbor, and I wanted you to know how much I appreciate your work."

More silence.

"I've been doing this work for twenty years, and no one has ever called to thank me for it," said Brant. "People only call me when they have problems." He was incredulous.

I had a similar experience with L.J., who sold me my car at the dealership. He answered my questions, didn't push, and gave me space to think and decide. I wrote to let him know that he completely exceeded my expectations of what a beat-'em-down car sales experience would be like and that I was happy with my car choice.

L.J. called me a few days later. He said that his was the first thank-you note in the history of the dealership. The managers open the mail and then pass on all acceptable communications to the sales team. Evidently, my note was circulated through the ranks, and as a result, L.J. was mercilessly teased. But I'll bet that every one of his peers looked at him differently after that.

I have now lived long enough to know what my mother knew as she encouraged her protégé to practice her thank-you-note scales: There is some alchemy that can happen despite us. It takes us through the fire of our resistance, through the abrasive discipline of our effort, until we arrive at something pure and true and so obviously authentic that was never before comprehensible.

I hated writing thank-you notes until I loved it. What I discovered along the way was that practice is not only the path to mastery but also a means of initiation into ourselves. Through the repetitive act of giving thanks, I discovered how deeply grateful and fortunate I am. As I wrote myself to a heightened state of gratitude, I became aware of the fabric of good fortune into which I was solidly woven—and this strengthened my bond with most of the people who crossed my path.

BE FIERCE

I listened to my mother because I trusted and respected her on matters of the heart and the word. This has shaped my character and informed my calling. Has someone you admire challenged you to try something in your writing life that you'd rather not try? What if you were to commit to it simply because they asked you to? It might be interesting to find out what awaits you on the other side of your discomfort.

GET TO THE PLACE OF GRACE

A piece of writing is organic material. It starts with the single cell of an idea, and then invents itself through our labored accompaniment into an expansion of blood and bones, eyelashes, the sweet in-and-out rhythm of breathing.

You probably prefer to think you know your writing intimately. It came through you, after all. You chose to make it, and you are in charge. Right? Until, like a young child, it wanders out of the house while you are sleeping, releases the car's emergency break, and rolls out into the middle of the intersection. Until it ruins the rug with nail polish. For the third time.

No matter how experienced you may be, each piece of writing arrives on its own terms, and you must learn to interpret its cries and give it what it needs. When and what to revise, if and when it is finished, and when to let it go into the world are questions whose answers must be sourced from the writing itself. It can be difficult to know, and much of what we writers do is trial and error (or, as I like to say, practice).

I once heard Judith Barrington advise a group of writers, "After therapy, the memoir," which I interpret to mean: do your personal work, come to resolution about your issues, and then tackle the story behind the struggle. I think the most common mistake we writers make is to hurry a piece of writing out of our hands and into the world before it is ready to go.

It is important to remember that a piece of writing is finished when both emotion and craft have come to resolution.

If a story or poem or manuscript or article is not yet finished with you, it is not finished—no matter how accomplished the work may be.

I was astonished at the fury of poems that poured through me during my divorce process. After about two years of writing and revising, I was on the brink of completing a poetry chapbook titled *How to Leave Your Husband*. I was smugly satisfied with the righteous rage and arrow of blame I had retrained from my ex-husband's heart to the page. A new, raw and unpretty voice had come through, and I was committed to letting her be heard.

However, once I considered the poems finished and the manuscript ordered, I couldn't seem to let it go any further than my office. Though I wasn't able to articulate it then, I now believe that I was still in the suspended, watery place in which writing happens. I hadn't come through to the dry land of objectivity in which poems dry their wings and build their nests.

As the manuscript sat for a few years, I settled. And when both of my feet were finally on the ground again, I pivoted. A new surge of poems came through to bring my manuscript to full book length. The tone of these poems reflected my new orientation: landed. My screechy voice softened. I moved from "broken open" to "stitched back to greater integrity" with humility and awe. There was a greater complexity of wound and gift interwoven in the language and imagery.

Tilting on a new axis now, this collection had outlived the edgy and somewhat flip title *How to Leave Your Husband*. The new anchor poem informed the new title I chose: *Holding up My Empty Hands*. At long last, my manuscript and I were finished.

Thankfully, my writing buddy Dave was close at hand when my memoir in the works—an investigation into my journey through C-section, miscarriage, and divorce— required a similar shake of the snow globe. I explained to him that my memoir's theme was inspired by the Mahaside quote "Barn's burnt down, now I can see the moon," and my working title was *Burning Down the Barn*. I was stuck and struggling, because I couldn't seem to write myself out of the burning barn. Dave proposed that I simply change the working title to *Now I Can See the Moon*. This changed everything.

In one swift maneuver, Dave helped me shift my focus from crisis to illumination. By simply reminding me that I was moving toward the moonlight, he turned around a story that was breech inside of me so that it could make its way through the anguished contractions of gratitude and insight and onward to where it needed to go. What I understood quickly after this re-orientation is that my story was actually about the surprising wellspring of self-love that these losses helped me discover and tap.

Of course, this kind of struggle is not exclusive to adapting personal experience to writing. Fiction, how-to articles, and strategic marketing copy are equally vulnerable to getting stranded in the unfinished place inside yourself. You have the same opportunity to authoritatively populate the landscape your writing occupies by closely listening, attentively writing and rewriting, and inviting trusted advisors to point out opportunities for course correction.

There is that moment in any piece of writing that I call lift-off. Where the sum is greater than its parts. Where craft is so refined and so aligned with intent that you introduce something undeniable that lives on inside of you and your readers. You know what it feels like in your body to get there. Even if it's only happened in small moments, you know what it's like to say something the way it was meant to be said, as only you can say it. When that triumphant plunk of "YES" rings through you.

Whatever it means to you in your life and your writing, be on the lookout for that lift-off in your words and that landing in your being. Hone your attention to the place of grace where you can feel, know, and trust that you and your piece of writing have completed your journey.

HAPPILY EVER DURING

I wonder which came first: the fairy tale or the human yearning for happily ever after? As a child, I remember being perplexed when stories of love fulfilled ended at the first kiss. How did the new couple manage to get along after they sorted out all of the rags-to-riches details, the glass shoes, the unconscious-in-a-forest-of-dwarves dilemmas, and other dramas that made the elusive prince so compelling and seemingly all-powerful?

In my early years I worshipped the poets and writers I loved to such an extreme that they seemed more mythological than human. Publishing a book in this paradigm was like a magic spell that could render the girl scrubbing cat vomit out of the carpet worthy of … what? Love? Existence? It seemed that somehow the approval of others, via my name on the spine of a book, had the power to make me a different, better person.

I was wrong.

As it turns out, I was the same old me after I'd written my first book—just a far more exhausted and terrified version of me. Having always written privately, secretly, for my own satisfaction, I suddenly had to face the fear of people actually reading what I'd written and having opinions about my work that were entirely out of my hands.

The report from the postpublication trenches seems to be universal: Having completed the Herculean task of writing a book, writers generally experience the postpartum emptiness of no longer writing, followed by the rest-of-your-life commitment to marketing the book. There's more cat vomit to be scrubbed, bills to be paid, diapers to change, and so on. Spoiler alert: Happily Ever After, as we imagined it, never arrives.

So what's the point of all this writing and publishing if it doesn't get us to the right ball or attract the attentions of the perfect prince?

As I see it, the real sweet spot in the writing life is Happily Ever During. What makes the writing life worthwhile is the way in which staying fiercely committed to our work lets us inhabit ourselves more fully.

When we are engaged in writing, no princes or balls are necessary. Everything we need is happening on the page, moving through our fingers. Our entire universe is contained and complete. No need to pine for some fantasy state of being, some pinnacle of accomplishment that we imagine is an improvement on the ecstasies of wrestling with language in the here and now.

Happily Ever After is a fantasy. And fantasies can be fun until you actually try walking in glass slippers. Even if you get exactly what you thought would make your life perfect, chances are good that your happiness is not as dependent on such an outcome as you might think.

Happily Ever During is reality. And you get to decide, moment by moment, how it's all going to go down. When you do, every unexpected harvest will be your own.

BE FIERCE

Are you moving toward a destination that you imagine will make life far better than it is today? If so, I invite you to consider how the *journey* is improving your life right now. As you strive for your treasured goal, consider whether you are already inhabiting the sweet spot.

CARS DON'T MELT

IF THE METAL DOESN'T BEND, DON'T HAMMER HARDER—APPLY MORE HEAT. —*Marc Lesser*

When she asked me what I was bringing my car in for, I told Wendy, the dealership's kind and helpful service support woman on the other end of the phone, that I wanted to replace the trim around the windows of my car because it had melted.

"Cars don't melt," she laughed. "I've never heard of such a thing in all my days of service. After all, it's not like we live in Arizona!"

"No one was more surprised than I was that a new car could melt," I said. "You can take a look and decide for yourself."

When I brought my car in, I explained to Wendy that when I'd noticed the first disfigured stripe across the hard plastic, I suspected foul play. But then a week or so later I discovered another stripe, and then another, all in a repeating pattern. I couldn't figure out what was going on until I noticed two stripes of burnt grass on my front yard that ran at the same angle as the stripes on my car.

I asked my boyfriend, Mark, who is trained as an aerospace engineer, if he thought the sun could be reflecting from some part of my house to burn the grass and melt my car. He confirmed that it was possible and pointed to the window he suspected was the culprit.

I started parking my car somewhere else—and arranged to bring my car in for service.

After a team of mechanics and service managers huddled privately around my car for a good long while, Wendy reported back from the service dock to confirm that my car had, indeed, melted.

As she started researching what it would cost me to replace the damaged parts, the hilarity of the situation finally caught up with me.

"Are you telling me that my new car melted, and I am responsible for paying for it?" I laughed, incredulous.

"Yes. This is not a manufacturing problem that's covered under warranty," Wendy explained. "It's like you parked too close to a fire; we're not responsible for that."

"But I was not parked anywhere near a fire. I was parked in front of my house. And my car melted."

Poor Wendy paraded out all of her best metaphors and similes to help me understand why the dealership could not accept responsibility for this damage. But I just couldn't take no for an answer. It made no sense to me that a car manufacturer would not replace a new part that didn't hold up with ordinary use.

Eventually the service manager agreed that they'd take photos, share it with my car's manufacturer, and see what they could do. I was reassured that it was 99.9 percent unlikely that they'd be able to cover the damage.

By the end of the day, I'd heard back from Wendy. The manufacturer was going to replace the parts at their expense.

I was thrilled about the good news, but even more thrilled about three important discoveries I'd made during this experience, all of which have informed my writing practice.

1. WHEN YOU SIMPLY CAN'T COMPREHEND THAT *NO* IS A POSSIBLE ANSWER, YOU ARE FAR MORE LIKELY TO GET A YES.

In this instance, I was so certain of my perspective that *no* had nowhere to land in me. As I drove home from the dealership, I considered: What if I were equally certain that it was time for my poetry manuscript to be in print? What if I simply couldn't imagine, couldn't *accept as reality*, that any publisher would reject it? What if its eventuality as a book were an absolute in my mind? How would this incredibly different vantage point about my creative work change the context and the results? I decided to experiment.

2. INTENTION + PASSION + DETACHMENT = FREEDOM.

At the dealership, I had a strong intention to have my car repaired at no cost. I also had a great deal of (nonrighteous) passion about it; my emotions were fully committed to this desire. Yet paradoxically, I wasn't particularly invested in the outcome. Meaning that if the dealership hadn't covered the melted plastic, I would have simply left well enough alone and moved on. No biggie.

As I drove away from the dealership having been reassured that there was almost no chance my desire would be fulfilled, I felt delighted and complete. Why? Because I had made my desire and my point of view completely clear in a friendly but firm way. I had left no part of it hidden or undisclosed. What happened from there was out of my hands. For me, fully asking for what I wanted completed our transaction. Whether or not I got what I requested mattered far less than how great it felt to ask.

I concluded that this is the ultimate freedom: wanting, asking, and then letting go. And, mysteriously, it seemed to make me almost magnetic to receiving.

3. FOCUSED LIGHT CAN MELT A CAR!

Most writers I work with fret about having enough time, energy, and resources to establish and sustain the writing lives they want. My car happened to melt when I was writing a book in the margins of running a full-time business as a single mom and enjoying my own epic resource stretch.

A small amount of focused light had *melted my car.* This event resonated in me as metaphor. I, too, could direct a small amount of extremely focused attention to transform pretty much anything. All that appeared fixed and impermeable was likely to prove far more supple if I committed to and engaged deeply with it.

My car had validated the premise that increased heat results in increased fluidity. I made a new commitment to myself to apply more heat to the areas of my writing life where I wanted better results.

BE FIERCE

Because I am not emotionally attached to my car's appearance in the way that I am invested in the quality of my writing, I was able to practice some new approaches and implement some important new strategies to move toward what I wanted without getting in my own way.

I managed to hold a laser focus that leapfrogged doubt and the wobble of worthiness. I simply went for what I wanted as if yes were the only answer—all the while unconcerned about actually getting the yes, because that part was out of my hands. And through this new freedom, I was double gratified: by the pleasure of making the request and by the pleasure of having it fulfilled.

How can you find similar freedoms as you turn up the heat in your writing life? What can you do to raise the stakes (and the flame) to melt your own resistance in the areas of your greatest desires and ambitions?

LOVE THE DOG YOU PICK

I was lying on the floor next to my dog Hamachi, rubbing her belly and crooning into her ear about how beautiful she is, what a wonderful friend she is, how much I love her. As she smiled and yowled back at me through her crooked little front teeth and her black-lipped snarl, I marveled that I had lived with this dog for twelve years and neither of us had ever uttered a comprehensible thing to the other.

If you live with dogs, you know that this language barrier doesn't matter. We affirm our affection and devotion through our daily charades of feeding, petting, walking, and intertwined sleep. Not only does it not matter that my dog and I can't talk to each other, it may be exactly *why* our love is so undeniable. When I shared this observation with my friend Dale, he elaborated: "You don't ever hear people asking, 'Did I choose the right dog?' We are just happy to love whatever dog we picked."

It's true: We don't tend to wonder what our relationship with our dog should give us, or worry that we could have had a better walk with a different canine. We just show up, day after day, year after year, and do what needs to be done to cultivate a shared love and a shared life.

Our writing lives can be this simple and uncomplicated—and can benefit from this same kind of unconditional devotion.

As writers, we have a tendency to doubt our choices, question our themes, reconsider our genres, and imagine that every writer on the planet is doing something more important, more impressive, more coherent, and more likely to result in success.

Well, guess what? I hate to burst your envy bubble, but you're not going to get any more important, impressive, coherent, or successful by being someone you're not—or by attempting work that you are not called to create. Doubting your commitment and your capacity, or wishing that you or your writing were something else entirely, will only keep you immobilized.

My whole life I have been consumed with making sense of how people evolve and heal in relationships with other people. This was once a source of humiliation for me. For decades, I yearned to write about the more "important" themes other people addressed in their writing. Then, after half a lifetime of writing what I couldn't help but write, I started to notice that the current of my deepest question, *How do we become our most authentic selves and live our best lives?*, was leading me to some surprising and life-changing revelations that deeply affected my readers and me.

In effect, I loved my writing so much that my doubt had little room to generate turbulence. Had I listened to my (very loud and quite insistent) inner critics, who were unconvinced that my theme of choice was worthy, I never would have arrived at the vistas of insight and liberation I've discovered along the way.

This is why I believe our job as writers is to welcome the writing we are called to do in the same way we love the animals in our lives: with everything we've got. To trust that the material we have chosen (or that has chosen us) is the path to our deepest riches. When love leads us, day by day, we can cultivate a practice through which our accountability to ourselves and our work becomes undeniable.

Let yourself be obsessed. Let yourself coo in your writing's ear and tell it that it is the most beautiful, the most perfect companion you could ever imagine. Know that it is the sound of your voice the writing loves, as well as the sound of your footsteps as you approach your writing chair. It waits for you in the lost place that is the unwritten page, one ear pricked, with the enormity of its single-minded desire to join you wherever you are headed next.

PRACTICE CLOSES THE GAP

IT DOESN'T MATTER IF ANYONE READS IT, BUYS IT, SPONSORS IT, OR SHARES IT. IT MATTERS THAT YOU SHOW UP. —*Seth Godin*

We write because we have something to say, and most of us spend our lives learning how to say it. When Ira Glass spoke in Portland years ago, he discussed the gap between the impulse to create and the ability to realize our vision. He shared an insight that he said he wished he could tell every artist and writer at the beginning of their journey: *Everyone who eventually makes great creative work first spends many years making mediocre work.*

Everyone.

The most important thing you can do for your craft, says Glass, is to create a huge volume of work. Just keep doing it and doing it and doing it. It's the only way to close the gap.

I agree with him completely.

Considering our craft as a lifelong discipline is a valuable point of orientation. But I think this insight is not enough to keep us writing. We need to be very clear about our motivation, and we need to call ourselves back to it every time we get discouraged, lost, or afraid.

If you think your motivation is to get published, I suggest that you dig deeper. Publishing may happen at some point on the trajectory, but the validation of the world is unstable ground on which to construct a writing practice. And the "success or failure" conversation can shut you down just when you're starting to secure your foothold.

Want a powerful way to change how you show up at the page and ensure that you stay with your writing practice for the long term? Here are a few suggestions.

ASK NOT WHAT YOUR WRITING LIFE CAN DO FOR YOU BUT WHAT YOU CAN DO FOR YOUR WRITING LIFE. We tend to think of the writing life as a workhorse, one that throws its shoulders behind our chosen goals and takes us where we want to go. However, the fierce writer looks at her writing life as a tender being she can give service to. What does the writing life need to sleep well and perform well, sink its roots, thrive? How can you ensure that it will entrust you with its secrets, its vulnerabilities, its uncertainties?

CAPTURE EVERY IDEA. One way to become more reliable to your writing is to get down everything that wants to come through. Whether you're in the shower, napping, driving, doing other high-stakes work, or washing dishes, create a simple system for capturing the images, phrases, or ideas that arise. In this way, you become a reliable witness to yourself, and you get in the practice of welcoming all that comes, whenever it comes.

I keep index cards everywhere: in my purse, my bedside table, my kitchen, my dog-walking bag, my car … I even have a special crayon I inherited from my son that I use to write down ideas on tile when I'm in the shower. Being prepared is invigorating. And accumulating evidence that I have something to say keeps me deeply engaged.

SCHEDULE TIME TO WRITE. Another way to show yourself that you mean business is to designate a regular time to write. Then do what you need to do to protect it—whether that's blocking out time in your schedule or barricading the door to the closet where you are hiding from your family as you write. Each time you show up for your scheduled writing time, you reinforce your reliability to yourself. You fortify your practice. In this way, over the course of a lifetime, you can transform writing practice into a biorhythm that you don't have to choose or even think about. It will become a natural way of moving through life.

WELCOME YOURSELF AND YOUR WRITING AS YOU ARE. Maybe the most important way to close the gap between mediocre to great is to adore the deep, messy, wobbly middle of your work and your writing journey in the same way you would love a child who has not yet mastered language or bike riding. When you stop thinking of practice as the road to perfection, you can let it be what it is: a journey full of unexpected plot twists, disappointments, celebrations, and revelations. Keep encouraging your risks, appreciating your falls, and honoring the undefined.

• • •

Practice closes the gap between mediocre work and great work. But it does much more than that. I think a writing practice is one of the greatest acts of generosity and compassion a writer can make. It teaches us to witness, and to reach beyond, the known and the bearable toward truth. It teaches us to flail about on the periphery of that truth until we land in the absolute presence of writing as its own reward. If you can stay right there—willing, wondrous, in service to the unknown—you will eventually close the gap between vision and realization.

You may find that your evolution as a writer gives you the kind of satisfaction you once believed could only come from publishing. And from this deeply resourced practice of satisfaction, opportunities you may never have expected will likely become possible.

BE FIERCE

Why do you write? What deep place in you is asking to be reached or expressed in words? How is writing essential to your happiness? How is it fundamental to your survival? I invite you to name and claim your deepest, truest, most vulnerable motivation. Write down your answers to these questions and keep them close at hand as you write. Living and writing by these truths will fortify you over the years. And it can help ensure that your writing practice is so essential that the obvious choice will be to keep writing and writing and writing. No matter what.

THE NET MAY OR MAY NOT APPEAR

GO TO THE EDGE OF THE CLIFF AND JUMP OFF. BUILD YOUR WINGS ON THE WAY DOWN. —*Ray Bradbury*

I'm a leaper. For better or worse (often for worse), I trust my instincts completely. When my gut says leap, I leap: groundless, in love with whatever I've surrendered myself to in that moment, and on my way to quickly and indelibly finding out if it loves me back.

At times I've felt ashamed of this. When I make terrible choices that hurt me, or come to conclusions that perhaps I would not have made if I had walked or crawled instead, I envy the slow deciders. The cautious and careful. The reasonable. Surely they didn't get up on stage to sing and screw it all up. Or take the wrong job. Or marry the wrong guy and end up alone with a two-year-old. Surely they don't follow their intuition all over creation just to land back home where they started. The slow movers must arrive somewhere significant and well planned, right?

Lately, I've taken a new position on my leaping tendencies. I've decided to accept that this is the way I am. It doesn't matter where the slow movers net out, because this is not my speed and it's not the way I'm going to move through life, no matter how much I might appreciate the advantages of a more cautious pace.

For better or for worse, my passions are huge, my movements are often dramatic, and I trust this way of being because it feels the most natural. My job as a leaper is to accept that risks are, well, risky. The net may or may not appear when I am in full-throttle motion. I can beat myself up about the fact that I'm free-falling in unknown territory, or I can build my wings on the way down, as Ray Bradbury suggests.

For me, the mandatory wing-building skills are gratitude, forgiveness, reckoning, and recommitment. Freedom is my primary value, and courage is the transportation of my choosing. I take risks that help me grow because I am willing to make mistakes, get hurt, look stupid, and disappoint myself and others.

The older I get, the more I wonder if the net is even the right thing to wish for. When we are moving at our natural speed, we lean into the opportunities and learn the lessons that are most aligned with who we are.

I don't know anyone who believes that they can do something before they actually do it. It's the blind leap that helps us discover the distance between us and our goals, the skills we need to cultivate to bridge the distance, and the tenacity to persist until we figure it out.

Every landing teaches us the art of flight, no matter how clumsy or difficult or ecstatic it might be.

BE FIERCE

How do you leap—and land? What are your wings made of? What are you willing to risk in your writing life, without knowing where it might take you?

STICKS AND STONES MAY BREAK MY BONES, BUT NAMES CAN CHANGE THE SHAPE OF WATER MOLECULES

At the White Eagle bar with some of my favorite poets after a reading, Jason spoke of the first time he was referred to as a poet and how this single reference planted the seed of identity he still carries today. I, in turn, recalled Mr. Cwanger, my sixth-grade teacher, who told me I was smart and gave me a ruler and a thesaurus with my name in it as a reward for reading the most books of anyone in his class. Mr. Cwanger's validation gave me permission to start seeing myself as someone capable of achieving.

As our conversations mingled in the drifting hum of smoke and friendship, I marveled at how the words of even a casual acquaintance can influence our direction and ability to claim our lives. Words can be the magic carpet that takes us beyond the limitations of our self-image, and they can be the cannon that sends our dreams spiraling down from the sky.

I was raised with the expression, "Sticks and stones may break my bones, but names can never hurt me." Like most things I was told about life, this proverb proved wildly inadequate in summarizing the complex ways in which we damage each other and ourselves. Bones heal, but names are absorbed. Most of us carry into adulthood any number of unkind words that are lodged in our softest places. Inside of us, hidden so as to protect us from further pain, these words gain influence: *Ugly, Fat, Stupid, Loser.*

Scar tissue starts to form around the words as the body rebuilds itself around the wound. Through this calcification process, the offending words are pushed deeper. Eventually the sore spot loses flexibility and feeling until we have lost a ligament or even an organ to a rejection we have made it our special mission to carry.

Dr. Masaru Emoto's book *The Hidden Messages in Water* explores how water molecules change under the influence of words. By presenting different written and spoken words and music to the same water samples, Emoto has documented how water changes its expression at the molecular level.

For example, water molecules that have been exposed to nourishing words such as *love* and *gratitude* show brilliant, complex, and colorful snowflake patterns. Water presented with *love* looks like an enormous diamond. In contrast, water exposed to negative words such as *defeat, rage, despair* forms incomplete, asymmetrical patterns with dull colors. The water crystals influenced by heavy metal music look to me like the head of a cymbal.

The common wisdom is that you are what you eat. Most of us consider how the fuel of food contributes to the evolution of our bodies and health. Given that we are composed of three-fourths water, could this mean that we are also three-fourths susceptible to the influence of words?

Perhaps it is equally possible that you are what you say (and what you hear).

When I proposed this to my friends at the bar that night, Gregory said he carried a briefcase (for his books) and a tuba case (for his tuba) in high school. The epitome of a nerd, he was teased mercilessly. Finally, Gregory decorated his tuba case with a bumper sticker that earned him a little distance from his aggressors. It said: "Don't laugh, mister. Your daughter could be in here."

First, this made me laugh. And then it got me wondering. This tacit duel of clashing words amounts to an eye for an eye: If you challenge my weak spots, I'll attack yours. What happens to the heart of a boy whose passion is papered over with bravado? How did this influence his music?

Words give us a way to retain, make sense of, and even transcend our experiences. Every kind word opens us up a little, and every unkind word closes some part of us down. Since we have the choice, why not find a way to use words to craft a lifeboat that will sustain what we value most?

BE FIERCE

That one moment of affirmation you give yourself or someone else could permanently influence the composition of your reality or theirs. The next time you're preparing to go public with some sentiment, think for a minute about how your words might change your life, your tuba case, the world.

FROM BREAKDOWN TO BREAKTHROUGH

ONLY ONE THING MADE HIM HAPPY / AND NOW THAT IT WAS GONE, / EVERYTHING MADE HIM HAPPY. —*Leonard Cohen*

I was about to start writing a memoir. I felt like I'd been circling the landing strip of this story for years but hadn't yet figured out how to align the machinery of my craft within the double-yellow lines of a meaningful narrative.

I signed up for a live storytelling class to shake things up inside of me. The terms of this class were to show up with an idea and, in the company of fellow class members, to spend six weeks talking it through and teasing it out into a meaningful and complete six-minute story. You couldn't write any of it down, ever. You simply practiced, experimented, got feedback, and refined. The culmination of the class was a live storytelling performance for a substantial audience.

I'd never told a story that I hadn't first written down. And I thought that entering an unfamiliar medium could be a potent way of exiting my own loop. I loved the idea of being in a beginner's state of mind and expecting less of myself—and therefore having more room to explore and discover.

I was instructed to bring a story with "heat," one in which I was unpacking something meaningful and vulnerable that would change my listeners and me. I chose a story that I hoped would distill the trinity of events that had permanently changed my life (C-section, miscarriage, and divorce) to a single, meaningful insight that could eventually become the organizing principle of my memoir.

I spent the first four weeks of the class in tears. I was swimming around inside the pain of the story but wasn't finding the breakthrough of insight or empowerment that would send me (or my listeners) up for air. I was surprised to find that there was still too much grief churning the deep silt of my being for me to see clear through to what needed to be told.

When one of the teachers suggested that I might need professional help instead of a storytelling class, I understood that I wasn't going to be telling this particular story in this particular class. The problem I was so passionate about solving would remain unsolved, for now.

I hate to quit. I value the growth and discovery that comes when life (and writing) are truly challenging. I had made a commitment to myself to tell a story to a live audience without a printed page. And I really wanted to follow through on it. However, by week five, I had to admit that the story I'd been working on was unredeemable. My teachers seemed convinced that I'd never emerge from emotion into insight, and I was fairly convinced of this as well. I gave myself permission to quit. This was something I'd taken on as a fun challenge, and when I considered the bigger picture, it was not a big deal that I hadn't succeeded. I went to sleep planning to let the teachers know the next day that they could count me out.

On my dog walk the next morning, I ruminated on what raw material I could take with me from this storytelling class to my memoir-to-be. Deep in thought about what I had gained from these life losses, a new idea presented itself: the story of changing my name. It seemed to have nothing to do with the story I'd been struggling to tell. But there it was: a topic that filled me with heat and vulnerability, as was our assignment. I spoke the first line that came to me, and for the rest of the dog walk, I kept talking as the entire story unspooled from me: why I chose a new name, what it meant to me, and how it had changed me.

After twenty years of digesting and integrating this choice and telling versions and snippets of how and why I came to be Sage, the story came effortlessly. While I had been struggling mightily to solve another story, this new narrative simply showed up and, without fanfare, broke through my sound barrier of self.

I knew this was the story I was going to tell.

I called my teachers and let them know that I'd be showing up to the second-to-last class with a brand-new story. They didn't think this was a good idea at all. After all, they had no reason to believe that I even knew what a decent story was, given all the pointless flopping around I'd done in the previous weeks.

They asked me to tell it to them over the phone, and I did. When they heard it, they agreed that it would soon be ready to tell—and that I could start over so close to our performance date. As we marveled that this story had presented itself through the fallout of the other, I was reminded that we often live alongside stories that serve as tributaries of self without understanding how they source the deep waters we are seeking.

I appreciated the slow ripening of identity as our stories are sculpted by time, failure, recommitment, and endless retellings. I appreciated how the fires of our greatest disappointments burnish truths that are waiting for us in the ashes.

This, of course, is the architecture on which literature is built. The characters often struggle mightily, and their evolution depends on conflict or breakdown. But the story never ends here. From the death of expectation, something fresh is born. A new choice or point of view or attitude is possible—and it's typically not what the character had in mind. Both the character and the reader are changed in the telling.

Things fall apart in life. We try, we fail—and sometimes our losses are epic. How we put the pieces back together defines who we become as people, as writers, as authors of our own story. When we seek the opportunity to move from breakdown to breakthrough, we align ourselves with the great arc of literature. And we can trust that if we don't like the way the story ends, we can keep telling it until it we find our way.

BE FIERCE

Are you experiencing a breakdown right now in your writing life? How can you use this disappointment to help you clarify what you will move toward next? What friend or colleague might help you find a new perspective that can help you break through? What if what you lost is much less important than the journey of discovery it sends you on?

PICK THE
LOW-HANGING FRUIT

My day job as a marketing communications writer involves quite a bit of business jargon. One of my least favorites has always been, "Let's pick the low-hanging fruit." Meaning, let's take an approach that requires the smallest effort for the greatest return. Until recently, doing what's easy seemed like a cop-out and a strategic sacrifice of what might otherwise be best.

But what I now understand about the dissonance between the low-hanging fruit and me is this: I have always, on a cellular level, taken offense to the idea that something worthwhile could be easy. That is, until the weekend when I spent a late morning with my son, my brother, and his boys picking the low-hanging fruit from their plum tree.

After dozens of years of urban living, I felt a kind of unprecedented ecstasy in having dozens and dozens of perfect plums drop right into my hands from the low branches. And though the collecting process was effortless, I had no idea what one does with dozens of plums. Oh, how I love a learning curve!

The next few days were spent researching recipes and rediscovering my baking powders, flours, and tins. I baked a plum cobbler and a plum upside-down cake. I fell in love with plums uplifted in butter, sugar, and gluten-free flour. And I discovered that "easy" is not the equivalent of "boring" or "stagnant." It is instead a surprisingly obvious and joyful path toward illumination. I, who have spent my life avoiding the kitchen as if it had wronged me in childhood, did not leave the oven and flour-dusted counters for days. Eventually, I began researching beet recipes for my latest harvest from my own garden, and I searched for ways to enliven meals with the mint that flirts its perfect, fuzzy leaves at me all along the edge of our deck.

In fact, I think the plum harvest got me a bit "pick the low-hanging fruit" crazy. My office was taken by storm with the impulse. I completely overhauled my submission system in about ten minutes, in a way that made me feel overcome with the desire to send out my work. Then I spent the next ten minutes submitting two batches of poems to two contests. I tackled every task on my to-do list that could be completed in less than a minute. I had a revelation about the trash can, the bookshelf. I got the envelopes out for a mailing I've been dreading. Somehow, having the supplies at hand made the effort feel far more doable.

In short, I allowed myself to do what felt easy and right from moment to moment. This gave me energy and enthusiasm. I wasn't struggling to make myself behave, accomplish, meet deadlines, or any of the various things I have a tendency to strictly embrace.

True, I could have forced myself to revise that pressing client FAQ in the ten minutes I dedicated to my submission binder. However, I believe I was far more efficient by doing what I was moved to do first. By the time I turned my attentions to the FAQ, I was high on the satisfaction of an orderly system that reflected my current goals and priorities. My basket was already full of the low-hanging fruit, and now I was able to stretch a bit higher, balance on my toes a bit longer. I completed the FAQ quickly and well.

The gift the plums gave me, beyond the many unforgettable desserts they became, is the understanding that nothing is simpler and more efficient than identifying and moving toward what is comfortably in reach.

What could you do in the next three minutes that would take your writing life just a breath closer to where you want it to be? Would you be willing to spend three minutes on it right now? How does it feel to trust yourself that much? To get your will out of the way ever so briefly and let another guidance system lead you forward? There is no taste in the world like plum upside-down cake. What low-hanging fruit is about to effortlessly land in your mixing bowl, and what will you make of it?

CUPID HITS AN ARTERY

I was standing in front of a class teaching one night when the little yellow index card fell out of my notebook. It said, "Cupid hits an artery."

Four words, and I was transported to a weekend four years ago that was a pivotal point in my life. Now, I think of that time as my poetry colonic. For two days straight, on a cliff overlooking the Pacific Ocean, I purged poem after poem of my dead marriage onto the page. It was my birthday and two months after my husband had moved out of the house. I was in that no-coherence cellular soup when the caterpillar has not yet reorganized into butterfly. And poems were my cocoon.

As I held the index card, I wobbled for a moment.

Then I marveled at the way a single phrase can be a portal to another time and place. A time capsule. Transportation. The way a single page of writing can alchemize poison into medicine. The way a scattering of words can organize a broken heart back into a person again.

Poetry has taught me how to think, how to navigate emotion, how to write, and how to live. It is the best company I've ever found in the mosh pit of the heart—and in the trenches of life. The discipline of striving to align words with truths is the most powerful doorway I've ever walked through. And before walking through, I've spent thrilling, anguished decades fumbling with the key at the threshold.

Maybe the most difficult thing to understand in the early years of writing is that the high point of the writing life may be just there: before we get that key in the lock. Moments or days or years before we cross over to that imagined arrival point.

It is the striving that refines us as humans and writers. And every so-called arrival is just another foothold into the mystery. We may pause an extra beat to take in the view, pat ourselves on the back, and feel the gratitude for how hard we've worked. And then it's time for the next step. And the next.

When cupid hits an artery, we can simply write it down and see what words come after that. We can trust the words as companions. They don't have to be perfect or even good. They just have to land on the page, as we land in our lives: one foot, one word, after the other.

This is what makes a writing life.

OH, THE PLACES YOU'LL GO

It took me a long time to understand why anyone would ever want to publish his or her writing. In the privacy of my teenage bedroom, I was entirely satisfied to write secret poems in my secret notebooks. After a decade of this private inquiry, I turned my gaze outward a bit and soon ended up in a graduate program studying poetry. Though I shared my classmates' obsession with translating experience into insight through the medium of poem, I was unable to relate to their impulse to share that translation with others.

Gerald Stern, one of my poet heroes, was my teacher for a semester. I asked him one day what he thought the point of publishing poems was. "To reach people, Sage," he answered. A chill traveled my spine. Of course. My attention—and my feeble ego—had been entirely trained on the publishing itself, not the eventuality that a published poem would be shared with and consumed by a reader. Nor had it ever occurred to me that I might have something of true value to offer to that reader.

Over time, I started sending out poems and essays and book proposals to various publications and markets, and some of those were eventually published. I started blogging, teaching, and lecturing as well. Reaching people became a secondary goal to reaching and better understanding myself.

One of my personal writing projects grew out of sponsoring a young girl in an orphanage in China for several years through an organization called Half the Sky. Every month, I received a progress report about Liling along with a photograph. The single paragraph of poorly translated English always read like a poem to me. Most months, I'd write a response poem, trying to find my way inside Liling's experience—this child I would never know, whose life was linked by a postage stamp to mine.

When Half the Sky asked its donors to contribute pieces about their experience to their newsletter, I sent in one of my poems. Shortly after the poem appeared in the organization's newsletter, I was notified that I'd be sponsoring a new child now instead of Liling—and that the reason for this change could not be disclosed. I feared the worst.

A number of months later, I was contacted by an American woman in the Midwest whose family had recently adopted Liling. She said she had read my poem in the newsletter, searched for me online, and sought me out to see if I might be able to share information about the child's early life.

By sending just one poem into the world, I kept the line between Liling and me alive. I rejoiced in knowing that this child had been welcomed into a loving family—and that I was able to share the small amount of information I had collected about her early years with her new mother.

Almost a decade later, when I was in the depths of grief and loss while moving through my divorce, I received an e-mail with a subject line that said, "Thank you for changing my life." It was from a man named Mantu Joshi, who said that he came upon my book *The Productive Writer* at the airport and read it in one sitting. By the time he landed, he had become convinced not only that he had a book to write but that he could find a way to write it—despite the incredible demands he faced in parenting two special-needs children.

And that is exactly what Mantu Joshi did. For two hours a week, for two years, he wrote *The Resilient Parent*, a collection of heart-expanding essays that speak courageously and generously about how to survive and thrive while raising children facing extreme challenges.

As the fates would have it, Mantu lives in the same city I do. His book launch reading was on a night when my son was with his father, so I attended.

Mantu's event was a reading and a benediction in one. I experienced a man using language to transmute the greatest vulnerabilities and terrors of the human condition into grace. *The Resilient Parent* is a book for parents of children with special needs, but it is also a book for anyone who has struggled to find his or her balance amidst extremely strenuous circumstances.

I do not have a child with special needs, but I am a parent. And I am a human. I wept through most of the reading, awed by the opportunities we have to steer our thoughts, feelings, and lives with the stories we choose to tell. And I went home with valuable discoveries about ways I was harming myself and my co-parent as we navigated our divorce process.

Clearly, I was not alone in my need for this book-length benediction. Within a few weeks of publishing, *The Resilient Parent* was already in the top sixty-five in the Kindle special needs category, and it quickly rose to the top ten. Right out of the gate, this book was changing lives. Expanding hearts. Saving families. Entire communities were buying it, sharing it, distributing it at conferences. Into the great void of heartbreak, shame, alienation, and struggle that so many parents face alone came this lighthouse of a book. I bought a copy for everyone I could think of.

In an interesting twist, Mantu told me recently that he wrote to thank me because a chapter in *The Productive Writer* advised him to be grateful to the people he found helpful along the way. I made an invitation, he accepted it, and together we discovered more than either of us ever expected.

My experiences with Liling and Mantu taught me that when we commit to reaching people, we do so in ways that we may have never predicted and often never even know. When I became willing to risk exposure by sharing my work, I learned that a single poem can bridge continents and weave strangers into a family. And I had the good fortune to meet a man who taught me that with two hours a week, as well as passion, purpose, and permission, we can spin raw experience into gold.

BE FIERCE

Oh, the places we go when we are willing to send our words into the world and pay attention to where they lead us. How will you transform your writing practice in just two hours a week? How can you change the world by sharing a piece of writing that helps you feel connected to what matters to you?

LEAVE A TIGER BEHIND

At a recent workshop, I had a conversation with a writer who was feeling uncertain about how much time she had left on earth and therefore panicked about how much writing she might not be able to complete.

I have such compassion for this writer, and for every writer. We all stand with the enormity of the unwritten at our backs as we blaze a glimmer of words onto the page in the small allotment of hours we are given—or that we take—in our wildly unpredictable lives. I think of this tension as a kind of chiaroscuro: the unwritten as negative space giving shape to the words that come forward in the light of our writing. We need both the shadow and the light to find our way.

A few years ago, when I decided to give up a business I had spent fifteen years building and become an employee at a marketing agency, I made an agreement with myself that my creative writing life would go on hold. All of it. The teaching, the blogging, the authoring of books, the poem writing. This felt in a way like telling my heart to stop beating. But I looked at it as a kind of hibernation. Part of my life would undergo a wintering so that I'd have resources available to cultivate another primary part. My priorities were very clear. I let go.

Which brings me to the Queen of Wands, the card I am almost always presented with when I pull tarot cards. The Queen of Wands teaches us about transformation. Her story is one of shedding selves. With each wave of reclaimed self, the Queen of Wands changes hair color and companion animal. She goes from blonde to brunette to redhead and is accompanied by panther, then cougar, then tiger. When she makes her final crossing of identity, her companion animal cannot change with her. She must leave it behind to remind her of where she's been, to punctuate her understanding that when we embrace the new, we must let go of the old.

I distill the Queen of Wands's story (and all of ours) to this one simple truth: Sometimes we have to leave a tiger behind. This is what the fierce writing life demands of us.

We will not get it all done. We will not end up the person or writer we thought we would become. We will lose hair and friends along the way. We will accept what comes. We will release what is leaving. And we will allow our writing to flicker in the darkness because it is what we are here to do.

I can feel that tiger pacing the water's edge, the Queen's hair blowing back in the wind.

After a fabulous year and a half of employment, I quit my job, resumed my business, and committed to a new path of writing and teaching work that is taking me deeper than I have ever traveled.

I miss the tiger. I bless the tiger. I trust it to its destiny, and myself to mine. I write.

BE FIERCE

What have you let go of, or what has let go of you, along the path of your writing life? Did you think you might not be able to live (or write) without it—and have you? What has this taught you about your evolution on the page? What are you now willing to let go that you never thought you could leave behind? What part of you needs to hibernate so the rest of you can thrive?

FROM IMPOSSIBLE TO INEVITABLE

AT FIRST DREAMS SEEM IMPOSSIBLE, THEN IMPROBABLE, THEN INEVITABLE. —Christopher Reeve

Living the writing life we want can seem as improbable as Philippe Petit's famed acrobatics on a thin wire between the Twin Towers of the World Trade Center in 1974. We're often hovering precariously between the edifices of personal and work commitments. And whether we are exhilarated or terrified by this third space of elevated expectation (the one that insists we also write), the fact is that simply getting words down on paper can feel like a daredevil stunt.

Thankfully, writing is not likely life threatening. On the contrary, it can be so life affirming that we become willing to organize the terms of our existence around it. The key, I believe, is where we fix our gaze. Philippe Petit saw only his successful arrival at the opposing twin tower. He could not afford to look down and consider his distance from the ground below or the dangers of falling. And neither can we. Like Petit, where we focus is where we land.

It seems to be the human condition to give our attention to what's in our way rather than what's working. The idea is that when we know the problem, we can focus on fixing it. But the reality is that when we tell ourselves that we don't have enough time, space, balance, energy, momentum, success, reams of paper, life insurance, or whatever it is that we think we lack, we cement ourselves right there: without enough. And it's hard to dig ourselves out of that hole.

I believe that if you are called to write, you already *are* enough and *have* enough of everything you need to become the writer you were meant to be.

When you stop focusing on what's in your way and simply keep your attention trained on the end goal of making the crossing (whatever your particular crossing may be), your perceived obstacles melt away. You tap into resources you may not have realized you had—and you find surprising ways to source more.

As Lewis Howes advises, "Successful and unsuccessful people do not vary greatly in their abilities. They vary in their desires to reach their potential." I agree completely. The one choice you can make to help you completely leapfrog any stuck or struggling place is to amplify your desire. You can decide to do that this minute, and it won't cost you a thing.

If desire is the engine that moves your dreams from impossible to improbable to inevitable, a commitment to evolution is the fuel. When you use everything that happens to inform your growth and your writing practice, you become the expert specializing in you. If you value growth and are tending your evolution, true losses don't exist.

Hardships and heartaches inform greater wisdom and become a source of strength and stability over time as you adapt them to strategies that serve you better. Whatever didn't work becomes a path toward finding what does. Each triumph is equally valuable because it gives you leverage for the next triumph—by underscoring the places where you are strong, the processes that serve you, and the strategies that prove effective.

Having a cheerleader and a role model doesn't hurt either. My mom never gave up once she committed to a creative project, and she never considered her desired goal impossible. She simply stayed at it until she succeeded, and she taught me to do the same. We broke down any difficulty to its component parts, and she advised that I start by focusing on step one, because looking in any other direction would send me reeling right off the high wire of desire.

Once I had groped my way one step up above the impossible, I had elevated myself just a smidge toward the improbable. Step by step, I started gaining on improbable until I eventually left it in the dust of the approaching inevitable. Microgoals were the path to the macro goal, and each microsuccess gave me confidence that I was resourceful, determined, and equipped for the journey I had chosen. This approach works for me still, and it can work for you.

When we focus on reaching our potential instead of something far more finite, such as, let's say, being published in *The Paris Review*, we open up the possibilities for how we might be successful—and satisfied. *The Paris Review* is one among endless publications that we might consider submitting to, and perhaps we can look at publication in general— or even publication in that market, eventually—as one possible reflection that we are growing toward our goals.

But maybe first we can take a leap toward our potential by signing up for a workshop on dialogue, or by attending a weekend writing retreat, or by finishing a piece of writing we've stalled on. After that, we can take the next logical step, and then the next.

My whole life I knew I wanted to write a book. For more than twenty years, I drafted iteration after iteration of myself, along with thousands of poems, essays, articles, and marketing communications, until I felt I had a reasonable command of my instrument, a book-length-worthy topic I wanted to share, the confidence to pitch it, and the know-how to make it happen. I was patient and persistent. I found support from generous and well-informed guides. And I eventually wrote myself there.

Your sense of writing identity will ripen alongside your writing skills. And your absolute commitment to improving, learning, and finding the form for what wants to come through will help you make the passage from impossible all the way through to inevitable.

BE FIERCE

Inevitable success starts with knowing what you desire and then holding your focus there. As you move toward what you want, seek out what you need to grow and appreciate your evolution each microstep of the way. You have enough and you are enough to become the writer you were meant to be.

INDEX

feedback, 125, 160–62

feng shui, 77

Fitzgerald, Zelda, 29

focus, 83, 86, 182, 197–98, 225

forgiveness, 205

Forleo, Marie, 48

form, writing, 184–86

Frankl, Viktor E., 61

freedom, 163–65, 197, 205

freewriting, 20–21

fun, 83

future, vision for, 172

generosity, 108–9

genre, 3, 184–86

Glass, Ira, 201

goals, 21, 92, 106–7, 151

   defining, 44–46

   passion for, 172

   plan for reaching, 11–13

   and success, 63–64, 66

Godin, Seth, 18, 139–40, 201

Goldberg, Natalie, 21

grace, 86, 190–92

gratitude, 7–8, 48–49, 115–17, 169, 172–73, 187–89, 205. *See also* thank-you notes

Griffin, Andy, 118

habits, 6–8, 67, 80–84, 181

Hafiz, 6

Half the Sky, 218–19

"Happily Ever During," 193–94

happiness, 24–26, 73–75

Happiness Project, The (Rubin), 14

help, asking for, 160–62

Henry, Todd, 102

Hidden Messages in Water (Emoto), 207

hope, 138–40

Howes, Lewis, 224

human experience, 121–22

ideas, 30

identity, writing, 166–67, 225

illumination, 92

image, public, 72

imagery, 130

imperfection, 88

improvisation, 23

incubation, 91–93, 121

inner critic, 179, 200

inner X, 73–75

insomnia, 59

instincts, 204–5

intention, 11–13, 21, 28, 79, 81, 92, 141–43, 197

interference, 81

internal editor, 22

intimacy, 89

Iny, Danny, 176

Joshi, Mantu, 219–20

joy, 24–26, 73–75

Joy Team, The, 184–85

Jung, Carl, 17

Kinnell, Galway, 98

Kooser, Ted, 87

kryptonite, 112–14

Kunitz, Stanley, 2

language, specificity of, 97–98, 130

leading, 176–77

learning, 4, 45, 176–77

Lesser, Marc, 195

letting go, 30, 76–79, 197, 221–22

life-work balance, 94–96

limitations, 9–10

lineage, literary, 56–57

literary tribe. *See* community

losses, learning from, 63

low-hanging fruit, 213–15

"making it matter," 50–52

manifesto, writing, 166–67

margin times, 58–60

marketing, 127–28

mistakes, 87–90, 116

momentum, 3, 67–69, 82

motivation, 82–83, 201–3

WRITER'S DIGEST

Is Your Manuscript Ready?

Trust 2nd Draft Critique Service to prepare your writing to catch the eye of agents and editors. You can expect:

- Expert evaluation from a hand-selected, professional critiquer

- Know-how on reaching your target audience

- Red flags for consistency, mechanics, and grammar

- Tips on revising your work to increase your odds of publication

Visit WritersDigestShop.com/2nd-draft for more information.

PRACTICE. POLISH. PERSIST.

A Writer's Guide to Persistence

BY JORDAN ROSENFELD

A Writer's Guide to Persistence is your road map through the rugged terrain of the writer's path. You'll discover advice and techniques for cultivating a fruitful, deeply meaningful writing life by practicing your craft, polishing your work, and persisting through even the toughest challenges. Your journey to publication and success may take a lifetime, but you can sow the rewards of writing with every step.

Available from WritersDigestShop.com and your favorite book retailers.

To get started join our mailing list: WritersDigest.com/enews

FOLLOW US ON:

 Find more great tips, networking and advice by following @writersdigest

 And become a fan of our Facebook page: facebook.com/writersdigest